IRELAND

IRELAND

TEXT BY DERVLA MURPHY

PHOTOGRAPHS BY KLAUS FRANCKE

SALEM HOUSE
SALEM, NEW HAMPSHIRE

····· Northern Irish border
〰 Province borders
— County borders

Text © 1985 Dervla Murphy
Photographs © 1980 and 1985 Klaus Francke

This edition first published in Great Britain by Orbis Publishing Limited, London 1985.

First published in the United States by Salem House, 1985.
A member of the Merrimack Publishers' Circle, Salem, NH 03079.

ISBN 0–88162–099–8
Library of Congress Catalog Card Number: 84–52820

Printed in Spain.

Contents

The Irish Jigsaw Puzzle

The outsider, newly arrived in Ireland, may not at once realize that he is looking at a jigsaw puzzle. He sees a tiny island, blessed with an astounding variety of natural beauty, where half the citizens are under twenty-five and many of the dwellings are brand-new. Soon he discovers that the Republic of Ireland has a shockingly high rate of inflation, a temperamental telephone service, an agreeable if capricious climate, poorly maintained roads, one of the highest unemployment rates in Western Europe, indifferent food, excellent fishing where the rivers and lakes have not been polluted, a conspicuous population of tinkers, an astonishingly talented rural amateur theatre, magical skyscapes like you get nowhere else, a unique national sport (hurling), prodigious quantities of litter including rusty car-skeletons strewn around beauty-spots, lively traditional music, architecturally boring small towns, a distinctive equine sub-culture based on hunting and racing, an intense pub life, and natives who occasionally seem crafty and mean in the busier tourist centres but elsewhere are generously helpful. Most of Ireland seems easy-going and uncomplicated – still a bit backward, but none the worse for that.

Only when you look into Irish minds do you notice the jigsaw puzzle. If its tray is joggled the pieces tend to come loose, which can confuse both visitors and natives. It could be said that human history is a factory for making jigsaw puzzles. But in most countries, where the tray has not been joggled too often or too roughly, the pieces eventually adhere

Inishmore, the largest of the three Aran Islands. These are the summits of a reef stretching out from the limestone Burren, which is separated by little more than five miles from Inishere. Many monastic remains are found on all three islands, recalling those Dark Ages when Irish monasteries were culturally 'the storehouse of the past and the birthplace of the future' for Europe, in Cardinal Newman's words.

permanently to one another and an integrated picture, known as a 'National Identity', replaces all the bits. In Ireland this has not yet happened, though many Irish like to pretend to themselves (and others) that it has. Perhaps it never will happen. Perhaps we should settle for what we have: not a straightforward unmistakable National Identity but something much more subtle, intangible, elusive. One might call it a National Essence, for want of a better phrase.

Most outsiders quickly perceive Ireland as 'different'. Depending on the purpose of their visit their temperament and chance encounters, they may find the Irish way of life endearing, romantic, comical, exasperating, relaxing, pathetic, inspiring, depressing – or even all these things at once. Some are baffled by its 'differentness', because in the cities so few obvious signs remain to distinguish Ireland from a rundown region of Britain. In fact, our National Essence is increasingly being concentrated *within* the people. For years I have been conducting a private experiment during visits to London. Studying faces in public places, I spot someone who looks Irish and test my hunch by asking them the way. In 95 per cent of cases they speak with a brogue. Yet there is no longer – if there ever was – an Irish physical type. My recognitions have nothing to do with features, colourings, physiques; they depend only on facial expressions (often 'the look in the eye') – that is, on what shows through of the essence within.

A hundred years ago Matthew Arnold was ineffectually fretting about Ireland, as kindly uncomprehending Englishmen have been doing for several centuries. In one long essay – *The Incompatibles*[1] – he brooded over the refusal of the Irish problem to go away. 'England holds Ireland, say the Irish, by means of conquest and confiscation. But almost all countries have undergone conquest and confiscation; and almost all property, if we go back far enough, has its source in these violent proceedings. After such proceedings, however, people go about their daily business, gradually things settle down and nobody talks about conquest and confiscation any more. The Frankish conquest of France, the Norman conquest of England, came in this way, with time, to be no longer talked of, to be no longer even thought of. The seizure of Strasburg by France is an event belonging to modern history. It was a violent and scandalous act. But it has long ago ceased to stir resentment. On the other hand, the English conquest of Ireland took place little more than a century after the Norman conquest of England. But in Ireland it did not happen that gradually all memory of conquest and confiscation

[1] *Irish Essays* Smith, Elder, 1882

Everything in Ireland, even the buying of a newspaper, is a conversational opportunity.

died out. On the contrary, the conquest had to be again and again renewed. The angry memory of conquest and confiscation, the ardour for revolt against them, have continued therefore to irritate and inflame men's minds. They irritate and inflame them still . . .

Many Irish nationalists would insist that the ardour for revolt was a natural response to English cruelty, greed, injustice and oppression. Yet there is little evidence that the Irish peasant, as distinct from the king or chieftain whose lands were seized, had a harder life, materially, when the English took over as landlords from the Irish. More likely the ardour for revolt was fuelled by a proud awareness of being different – as the Normans were not different from the English, or the Alsatians from the French – and by a determination to remain different and a longing to be free to express that difference.

In December 1966 I landed at Dublin Airport twelve hours after leaving Nepal. For six months I had been working with Tibetan refugees in a Himalayan valley hundreds of miles from the nearest motor-road. In Katmandu, on my way home, I observed the authorities trying to cope with the cosmopolitan vanguard of what was soon to become an invading army of hippies and junkies.

From Dublin I hitch-hiked to Fermoy, Co. Cork, and by eight o'clock that evening I was walking towards a friend's house along a deserted country road. It was a 'grand soft evening' – our way of describing winter weather that is mild and moist. Through the bare branches of tall wayside trees – beech, oak, elm – a full moon was visible, flirting with thin silvered cloud. The nearest village was miles away, the stillness was broken only by the distant bark of a farmyard dog and the gentle rush of the Blackwater river, hardly twenty yards from my road. I absorbed that silence with joy, marvelling at its quality. Himalayan valleys are not noisy places, but this Irish silence was *different*. If sound, or its absence, may be described as something physical, Ireland's silence, at certain times in certain places, has for some a non-physical dimension: it can seem like a bridge to another time, or another world. More prosaic folk ascribe its peculiarity to Ireland's geographical situation as a small island on the edge of a continent – responding to an ocean, not to a land-mass.

Then suddenly – walking beneath those trees, by the river – I was conscious as never before of Ireland's remoteness, both in miles and in thoughts, from the rest of the world. Irish insularity has long been a

Enjoying rounds of Guinness in a County Clare pub. The Irish custom of buying rounds can disconcert foreigners. It means that if you are one of a party of six or eight, you cannot escape without sinking five or seven drinks: and if you were Irish it would be six or eight drinks. This tradition is party to blame for Ireland's high rate of alcoholism.

Hunters being discussed at Ballinasloe Horse Fair. The lowest price will be around five or six hundred pounds. The chestnut with the white blaze is likely to fetch several thousand. Thackeray found that in Ballinasloe beggars were 'more plenteous and more loathesome' than elsewhere.

Raking hay near Costelloe, Connemara, one of the few regions where such tasks are still done by hand. Connemara's population is mainly concentrated on the fringes of bogs and the lower slopes of mountains, and by the coast. One of the few remaining Gaeltacht areas, where the majority habitually speak Irish, survives on this Connemara coast.

subject of jokes, theses, pity, envy or, on the part of some Irish, self-congratulation. But that evening I *felt* it, as something palpable and enormously important: not to be condemned or applauded, but to be wondered at.

Most of my compatriots would then have regarded Nepal as a place almost unimaginably isolated. Yet to me, newly home, it seemed far more at the centre of things, and more influenced by outside events, than my own little country. In the valleys along the Tibetan-Nepalese border rumours abounded about the infiltration of Tibetan refugee camps by the CIA, and by Chinese and Indian military spies. It was hinted too that US Peace Corps volunteers, and Swiss, Australian and Israeli 'technical experts', and Japanese and German mountaineering teams were perhaps not quite what they seemed. The Chinese conquerors of Tibet were then building the Lhasa-Katmandu 'Friendship Highway', to join up with the Katmandu-New Delhi Rajpath, and there were sinister mutterings about this road being wide enough to take tanks. In the capital complicated espionage games were being played by a diplomatic community that saw the Mountain Kingdom's apparent innocence and non-alignment as a useful screen. Every day some detail reminded one of the East-West confrontation and what has since become known as the North-South imbalance. But in Ireland the outside world, with its gross extremes of riches and poverty, its conflicts and spies, its development schemes and racial tensions, existed only as newspaper headlines or pictures on television. It made no more impression on the average citizen than a film or a novel. Real life was what happened on our own small island and intrusions of larger realities from outside were instinctively repelled. This, it may be said, is a characteristic common to all conservative, relatively isolated societies. But in the twentieth century, in what we so oddly describe as the 'civilized world', the Irish have been singularly successful at defending themselves from such intrusions.

Afterwards, I realized that on that December evening, having spent most of the previous four years in other lands, I encountered my own country objectively for the first time. It was a good homecoming. AE (George Russell) had words for it:

> *I who have sought afar from earth*
> *the Faeryland to meet,*
> *Now find content within its girth*
> *And wonder nigh my feet.*

The village of Glencolumbkille, in a quiet valley in County Donegal. The name commemorates St Columba, known as Columbkille, a sixth-century monk who founded several monasteries, including Iona, one of the most famous centres of Celtic Christian scholarship. In our day Glencolumbkille is famous for its Folk Museum, its home-weaving and Ireland's first farming co-operative.

Dunluce Castle, County Antrim. There are many traces on this site of early Christian and Viking occupation. The first castle was built in the thirteenth century and later became a MacQuillan fort. Part of its supporting cliff collapsed in 1639, taking with it into the sea a section of the living quarters and eight servants.

An Atlantic mini-storm near Doolin, County Clare.

Left: *The Rock of Cashel was the Munster capital of King Cormac in the fourth century and became an important Christian centre in the fifth century. The thirteenth-century church was burned twice. Almost certainly there was a Celtic settlement on this site.* **Above:** *Cormac's Chapel on the Rock of Cashel was built 1127-34 and is the most remarkable Romanesque church in Ireland.*

Left: *The ruins of Jerpoint Cistercian Abbey – founded 1180, rebuilt in the fifteenth century – near Thomastown, County Kilkenny. The skillful and slyly humorous carvings of the cloister have been likened to relief illustrations for the Canterbury Tales.* Above: *Bishop's sarcophagus in Jerpoint Abbey.*

Ireland has recently been described by Professor L. M. Cullen as 'the last Western European country to abandon the medieval world'.[1] This was scarcely surprising since Irish medieval society had never formed part of the Western European jigsaw. It was based on a system of lineages within expanding clans unknown elsewhere in Europe, though common in Africa and Asia. Throughout most of Christendom, whether Latin or Orthodox, Christianity provided the framework for the entire social system, thus creating a fundamentally unified and coherent civilization whose members, whatever their racial differences, could understand each other's view of the world. But Celtic Christianity had developed in isolation (as had the Coptic Christianity of highland Ethiopia, another idiosyncratic outpost of Christendom) and it operated only on the spiritual level, leaving such matters as marriage and divorce to be controlled by the secular authorities, if at all. The clergy enthusiastically joined in the various tribal wars and battles, and also organized their own assassinations and faction fights over successions to ecclesiastical benefices. Ireland's wealthy hereditary clerical families – an unmarried Irish priest was exceptional – scandalized the outside world. As a result strenuous attempts at reform were begun in the twelfth century, when St Bernard of Clairvaux praised the labours of his close friend St Malachy, an Armagh man then striving to raise the moral tone of the monastery town of Lismore. The formidable St Bernard wrote: 'When he began to administer his office, the man of God understood that he had been sent not to men, but to beasts. Never before had he known the like, in whatever depth of barbarism: never had he found men so shameless in their morals, so wild in their rites, so impious in their faith, so barbarous in their laws, so stubborn in discipline, so unclean in their life. They were Christians in name, in fact they were pagans.'

The reforms initiated at the Council of Cashel in 1101 eventually achieved quite a lot. Yet as late as the first half of the sixteenth century many of the clergy were still vigorously breeding. Most discouraging of all to the reformers, some of the Anglo-French monks who had been imported to spread a knowledge of the new Canon Law, and cool the Gaels' ardour by setting a good example, had themselves taken to procreation in a big way.

There was no university in medieval Ireland, though there were many monastery schools run on individualistic lines by learned monks, most of whom were laymen. Among the minority who went abroad to study,

Previous pages: *Rosserk Franciscan Abbey on Killala Bay, County Mayo, founded in 1441 by the Joyces, and one of the best-preserved ruins in Ireland. Nearby are the ruins of Moyne Abbey, another fifteenth-century Franciscan house.*

[1] *The Emergence of Modern Ireland 1600-1900* Batsford, 1981

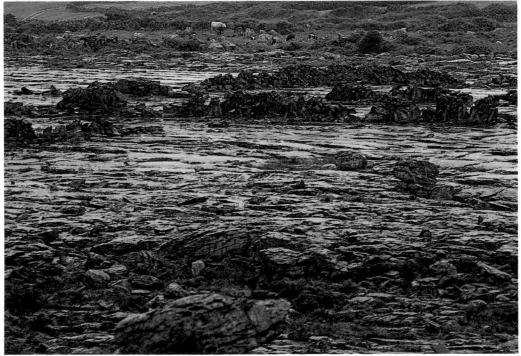

Top: *Autumn landscape in the Wicklow Mountains. Fertile hilly country alternates with deep glens.* Above: *The Burren, in County Clare, covers 160 square miles and its bare grey limestone slabs are without trees, soil or visible water. Yet between those slabs is to be found a variety of wild flowers and plants unique in the British Isles.*

Top: *Some of the Burren's several hundred species of alpine and Mediterranean plants.* Above left: *Heather on white stone near Malin Head, County Donegal, the northernmost tip of Ireland.* Above right: *Autumn colouring in south-west Kerry.* Right: *Glencar Waterfall, near Lough Melvin, County Sligo.*

Left: *Dolmens on the Burren. These graves usually consist of three to six upright stones, supporting a single stone slab.* Top: *In the ancient churchyard of Caldragh, at the western end of Boa Island on Lough Erne, sits this weird figure, which is probably pre-Christian.* Above: *Stone with prehistoric scribings at the entrance to New Grange, County Meath – Ireland's royal Bronze Age cemetery.*

Oxford was the most popular university. Those Gaelic students were, it seems, a turbulent lot; an Oxford statute of 1413 unsuccessfully tried to reduce their numbers.

In the fifth century Celtic Christianity reached a comfortable working agreement with the pagan gods and goddesses of Druidic times, and with the various Celtic spirits who occupied the rivers, mountains, forests and springs of Ireland. (I write this within a few hundred yards of one such spring – also in the monastery town of Lismore – from which blessed water is still taken annually on 14 May.) Ireland had experienced nothing like the early Christians' embittering struggle for survival against the mighty pagan establishment of Rome. It therefore seemed both expedient and charitable to allow a certain amount of compromise with the old beliefs: as happened in eighth-century Tibet when Buddhism supplanted the animism of the Bon-po, and in nineteenth-century Madagascar when Christianity supplanted the animism of the Merina people.

The archaic inauguration ceremonies of the Gaelic chieftains survived more than a thousand years of Christianity with their pagan spirit intact; a Connaught chief's accession was regarded as a wedding between king and kingdom. In such ceremonies the clergy participated increasingly towards the end of the medieval period, yet their presence entailed no modification of the pre-Christian rites. Everywhere a white rod was placed in the hands of the new ruler, usually by his chief vassal who also put on the king's shoe. All inaugurations took place on sites held sacred since pagan times, where the chief stood during the ceremony on a sacred stone. Queen Elizabeth I's general, Lord Mountjoy, has not yet been forgiven for shattering 'the stone of the kings' at Tullaghoge, on which the O'Neills of Tyrone had been inaugurated for generations beyond counting. In the Gaelic territories these ceremonies were held until the end of the sixteenth century.

The learned professions were hereditary in Gaelic society, though individuals could and often did practice more than one. The leading jurists, physicians, historians, scholars, harpers and poets enjoyed wealth and prestige and were exempted from military service and the payment of land-tributes – an admirable practice partially revived in 1969 by the Irish government when it exempted painters, musicians and writers from income tax. The chief poet of a territory was entitled to claim as his fee the wedding garments of every woman married within that territory. This immemorial Indo-European custom was a valuable

Giant's Causeway, County Antrim.

perquisite. The kings and nobles changed their spouses as often as (if not more often than) their clothes; and because divorce was easy a woman might have four or five weddings.

It was among a poet's many duties to glorify the often inglorious deeds of his overlord and urge him on to gain further distinctions – and, incidentally, loot. After a successful cattle-raid, inspired by literary eloquence, the poet could expect a share of the captured herd, which explains why the English authorities within the Pale proscribed 'rogues, vagabonds and poets' all in one breath. This tradition still re-echoes throughout contemporary Ireland. Emotional 'rebel ballads' form an integral part of the illegal Republican sub-culture and are immensely popular, even in impeccably law-abiding circles. Within days of any 'heroic' effort – the successful ambushing of British soldiers, the escape from jail of IRA prisoners – new ballads are being sung to glorify the 'heroes' and encourage further feats of endurance and daring. Nowadays such versifying is known as 'incitement to violence'.

The duality of medieval Ireland's religion is proved by another of the poet's roles. He was not simply a man who wrote verse but the Celtic equivalent of a witch-doctor – almost a shaman. Being universally regarded as a sacred personage, he enjoyed immunities at least equal to those of the clergy. His versified curses, mistaken for 'satires' by the English, were intended to injure or kill; numerous cases of 'poet's miracles' are recorded, when these curses were believed to have taken effect. One such victim was a Lord Lieutenant of Ireland, Sir John Stanley. The power of the poet's curse and the power of the Church's excommunication were habitually invoked together, without any sense of incongruity, against those who violated treaties.

Henry II's papal permit to annex Ireland did not lead to instant subjugation, and the Norman invasion and settlements cannot properly be described as a 'conquest'. Centuries of warfare followed, during which most of the newcomers were assimilated into the Gaelic world and much lost territory was recovered by Gaelic chiefs. Despite technical English overlordship, real power came to lie either with the semi-autonomous Norman-Irish lords, who dominated the east and south, or with the autonomous Gaelic chieftains, who still ruled over the west and north. The English administrators were confined to the Pale, a coastal strip around Dublin some thirty miles wide and forty miles long. Henry VIII's State Papers suggest that this region was defended by a stone and wood equivalent of the Iron Curtain.

Skellig Michael, County Kerry, one of a group of rock islets (Skellig Michael, Little Skellig and Washerwoman's Rock) which can be reached only in calm weather. To mark the dawn of Celtic Christianity, St Michael cornered many of Western Europe's high rocky places. Monks settled on Skellig Michael when their brethren were settling on Mont St Michel and St Michael's Mount in Cornwall.

Fear rather than greed prompted the decisive Elizabethan invasions, in the 1580s and 1590s, of what could so obviously be a useful military base for England's enemies. The colossal cost of these campaigns is now generally accepted as one of the main causes of England's Civil War. By the mid-seventeenth century the English administration had for the first time become effective over the whole island. Two later, long-drawn-out and no less ferocious campaigns, in the 1640s and early 1650s, and in 1689-91, completed the conquest. At that stage greed *was* an extremely powerful motive. By 1700, 27 per cent of the population of Ireland was of English or Scottish origin (as compared to 2 per cent in 1600) and six sevenths of the land had been taken by force from its rightful owners. Pax Brittanica had arrived. As Margaret MacCurtain has written: 'One system of law operated and in general was obeyed ... The country settled down to a long century of public order which concealed from the rulers the passions and aspirations of the ruled.'[1]

At the time of the Elizabethan invasions Ireland had few villages, never mind towns. Dublin was only slightly bigger than Drogheda, Kilkenny and Waterford; Galway, then an important merchant city, was the only town of any size on the west coast. The Irish export trade – mainly wool, fish and hides – seems to have been prehistoric rather than medieval. In 1394, when Richard II landed an army at Waterford, one of his French companions, Creton, was appalled by the low standard of living and the lack of efficiently organized work-forces. Yet Waterford and Dublin – both Viking foundations – were Norman Ireland's most progressive towns. The Elizabethans found things not much changed; indeed, because of constant turmoil throughout the sixteenth century, conditions had in some ways deteriorated. The situation was further confused by the sometimes overlapping operations of two systems of land tenure: non-feudal Gaelic and feudal Norman-Irish.

Landowners lived either in long single-storey thatched houses or in tall stone Norman tower-houses. Many of the latter remain scattered about the countryside to this day; they were still being built during the first half of the seventeenth century and still being lived in by Anglo-Irish gentry until the mid-eighteenth. Peasants lived in one-roomed chimneyless thatched cabins and cattle were their wealth; they had little furniture and few domestic possessions. Hence their habit – baffling and infuriating to the new English landowners – of simply disappearing overnight if they could not pay the rent, or for some other reason felt like a change of scene. In 1583 the Bishop of Meath – quite a prosperous

[1]*Tudor and Stuart Ireland* Gill & Macmillan, 1972

Little Skellig from Skellig Michael. **Overleaf:** *A bishop leading a group of pilgrims through the ruins of Clonmacnoise. This monastery, the greatest centre of Irish art and literature, was founded in 548-49 by St Ciaran, son of a chariot-builder from Antrim. By the twelfth century it was a miniature city, and its scriptorium produced many major works of Gaelic scholarship.*

region – made a will leaving the use of his best cooking-pot to the poor of Dunboyne and giving instructions about the settlement of those disputes bound to arise when selfish families tried to keep it too long.

Some argue that the remarkable paucity of artefacts in medieval Ireland was owing to the chronic instability of Gaelic society. True, the historians of the period record an almost permanent state of tribal warfare. Yet *all* the Gaels cannot really have spent *all* their time fighting, plundering each other's herds and crops, and burning each other's monasteries and settlements. Although Gaelic annalists disregard the more humdrum aspects of life, the ordinary folk must surely have known intervals of peace long enough to make everyday artefacts, if they were so inclined. The craftsmen of other European societies, regularly afflicted by invasions, revolutions and plagues, were not deterred from servicing their communities. It does seem that the non-aristocratic, non-learned Gaelic masses were content to live at an extraordinarily primitive material level, channelling all their creativity into song and story.

Fifty years ago Jung wrote, 'Everything we think is the fruit of the Christian Middle Ages . . . which lives in us and has left its stamp upon us for all time and will always form a vital layer of our psyche, just like the phylogenetic traces in our body. The whole character of our mentality, the way we look at things, is also the result of the Christian Middle Ages; whether we know it or not is quite immaterial.' If this is true, Ireland's aloofness from Western Europe during those centuries is sufficient explanation for our persisting 'differentness'. (It was aloofness, rather than isolation; there were many contacts, but the Irish chose to go their own way.) We have been fired in another crucible; at the level of a 'vital layer of our psyche' we are still a little apart from the rest. Despite the eventual transformation of Irish Catholicism into the very antithesis of Celtic Christianity, despite the loss of our language, despite centuries of intermarriage with settlers, despite our present hideously apparent relish for the trivialities and degradations of 'consumerism' – despite all that, 'the way we look at things' in the 1980s is, somehow, not quite like the way other Europeans look at them. Our leaders' post-Independence efforts to revive Gaelic culture failed utterly, yet the hallmark of that culture has not, it would seem, been entirely worn away.

I have occasionally recalled Jung's comment in another context, when travelling through the remoter regions of Afghanistan, Nepal, Ethiopia,

Slea Head, County Kerry, in the Gaeltacht area of Dunquin.

Turkey, Baltistan, Peru or Madagascar. Such places arouse in me a strong 'at home' feeling, a sense of being in harmony with my surroundings at a very deep level. Put in words, this can sound like frivolous (even callous) romanticism, a sentimental glamorizing of other people's poverty and backwardness because one gets a kick out of sharing 'the simple life' for a few months. But I sometimes wonder if my reaction to primitive societies is not in fact what Jung might call a phylogenetic response to the familiar – to what was, until relatively recently, my own ancestral way of life. In genetic terms a few centuries is a very short time, and four hundred years ago even the better-off Irish were living a life so simple that Captain de Cuellar – a Spanish Armada officer ship-wrecked on Ireland's west coast – described them as 'savages', using the word in no derogatory sense, but as an anthropologist might when describing the people of a materially primitive civilization.

In the 1960s there still remained one corner of my own land where I also experienced, in a somewhat attenuated form, this curious 'at home' feeling. An English friend had introduced me to the Aran Islands of Inishmore, Inishmaan and Inishere, off the Connemara coast. She and an eccentric Dane were the only foreigners who then owned property on the smallest island, Inishere – if property is not too pompous a word to describe their simple dwellings. I wrote two books, by candlelight, while sharing my friend's cottage throughout dramatically beautiful Aran winters, with the Atlantic raging mightily below our tiny windows. Sometimes it raged so mightily and for so long that we were cut off from the mainland for over a month and ran short of supplies. But in normal weather the *Naomh Eanna* arrived twice a week from Galway City.

There was a special excitement about boarding that little steamer for the voyage into Aran – a journey in time as well as in space. On Inishere there were then no motor-cars, no television sets, no daily newspapers, no telegraph poles or electricity wires – none of the outward (and few of the inward) signs of a 'developed' country. Water had to be fetched from the nearest well and the one pub-cum-shop was more pub than shop. Many of the 300 or so inhabitants still produced their own garments: for the women long homespun skirts and shawls, for the men loose bawneen trousers and jackets, heavy sweaters and floppy tweed caps. The narrow 'roads' were sandy or grassy laneways, between dry-stone walls, and the soil was innocent of chemicals. As the islands' natural surfaces consist mainly of bare limestone slabs, the islanders have been making their fields for centuries by spreading donkey-loads of sand and

St Cavan's church on Inishere. The date of this chapel is uncertain. It measures 24 ft by 12 ft and is surrounded by a modern cemetery. It is half-buried in sand which elsewhere on the island has completely covered similar ruins, but is considered holy enough to be regularly excavated. St Cavan's grave lies north-east of the church.

seaweed in alternate layers. Potatoes and rye (for thatching) thrive on this humus, and sheep and cattle do surprisingly well on the short, herb-strewn pastures.

The *Naomh Eanna* could not berth at either of the smaller islands so all goods and passengers had to be ferried to and fro in a fleet of curraghs crewed by long-faced, big-nosed, straight-haired men wearing cow-hide pampooties –a form of footwear designed to be improved by immersion in salt water. Traditionally, curraghs were made of cow-hide on a bone frame; now they are made of tarred canvas on lathes. Their design has not changed for millenia and the islanders construct them without benefit of gauge or rule, the required skills being cultivated by and passed on within certain families. Their very frailty enables them to survive in the most fearsome seas. When Robert Flaherty was making his famous film, *Man Of Aran*, in the thirties, several curraghs tackled forty-foot breakers as they raced through Brannock Sound off the north of Inishmore. But Flaherty cut that scene arguing that no audience would accept it as genuine.

Ireland has a strange effect on some otherwise sober imaginations and many foreigners travel misty-eyed into Aran, fancying these islands to be the last refuge of 'the pure Gael' – a creature unlikely to have survived anywhere into the twentieth century. Disillusion and confusion are the fate of such Gael-hunters when they discover that the Aran Islanders, despite their habitual use of the Irish language, are genetically no less mongrel than the rest of us. Their little piece of the jigsaw was given its unexpected character in the seventeenth century, when the islands were of strategic importance to England. An English garrison was maintained there for several decades – and married quarters were not provided.

During the 1950s two teams of physical anthropologists feasted on Aran blood and published the information that 'the blood group ratios in Aran, ABO, differ markedly from the adjacent counties Clare and Galway, coming much closer to the proportions found in the eastern counties of Wicklow, Carlow and Wexford, and still nearer to those of the north of England, where Saxon and Gael have probably mingled and intermarried for centuries. Again, the Rh factor occurs in different proportions to that of the adjacent mainland; and the teeth of Aran children appear to resemble those of London children'.[1]

Whatever about their teeth or their Rh factors, the islanders retained links with the Celtic and pre-Christian past long after these had been broken on most parts of the mainland. Close to our Inishere cottage was

Fishermen of Inishere. The man on the right is wearing the traditional cowhide pampooties, which are improved by frequent immersion in salt water and dry quickly on the feet.

[1]Daphne Pochin-Mould *The Aran Islands* David & Charles, Newton Abbot, 1972

Top: *Islanders carrying a curragh along the quay at Inishmore. J. M. Synge, who drew much of his inspiration from Aran life, wrote, 'A curragh with two light people in it floats on the water like a nutshell, and the slightest inequality in the stroke throws the prow round at least a right angle from its course.'* Above: *Men of Inishere receiving supplies from the mainland off the steamer* Naomh Eanna.

Beached curraghs on Inishere, the smallest of the three Aran islands. The ruin in the background is O'Brien's Castle, a fifteenth-century tower set in a ring-fort.

*The wreck of the **Plessy**, which on 8 March 1960 came to rest forever on the south coast of the Aran island of Inishere. She was already in a poor state and was driven ashore by the gales of that particularly stormy month.*

The Naomh Eanna *off Inishere. She cannot berth at either of the smaller islands and all goods and passengers have to be ferried to and fro in curraghs. Cattle are swum out to the steamer, then hoisted aboard by crane. When several animals are being exported to Galway fair there can be very long delays as they do not all take kindly to aquatic sports.*

Dun Conor Fort, on Inishmaan. The massive ramparts have wall-chambers and enclose a number of hut-sites; unfortunately much clumsy restoration work was done during the 1880s.

Dun Aengus Fort on Inishmore, the largest of the Aran Islands. This is one of the finest and most mysterious prehistoric remains in Western Europe. It covers eleven acres and stands on the edge of a 300 ft cliff overhanging the sea; part of the outer wall has disappeared owing to erosion. Nobody knows when or why in this forsaken place such a mighty fortress was erected.

the tiny church (twenty-four feet by twelve) of St Cavan, constantly threatened by the surrounding sand-dunes but considered holy enough to be regularly excavated. (There must be many more such ruins buried on the three islands.) St Cavan's 'pattern', held annually on 24 June, recalls the patterns (the word is derived from 'patron') once held in every Irish parish. As the night wore on the pagan origins of these festivals tended to become rather obvious and they were discouraged when Irish Catholicism was being drastically 'Romanized' in the nineteenth century.

I have not revisited Aran since 1968. In 1970 Aer Arann began a regular daily service from Galway City and by now tourism has become a major source of income. Not all the Aran sweaters and 'crioses' (long brilliantly dyed hand-woven belts, traditionally worn by Aran men) sold at high prices in the new souvenir shops have been made in Aran; and the shearing, spinning and weaving of wool for home use have been abandoned. Many donkey-carts have been replaced by EEC-subsidized tractors, though most Aran fields scarcely allow space for a tractor to turn around. Despite the provision of an Irish-language radio and television service in 1972, the mass-media are threatening the survival of Irish as the everyday language. And the islanders, once famed for their story-telling gifts, watch soap-operas on The Box. Twenty years ago the English spoken on Inishere was superb: original, vigorous, colourful, precise, with a distinctive rhythm of its own. Now, I'm told, it has become debilitated – infected by the DJ virus.

Of course all this is Progress – is it not? – and our modern gods decree that we must commend it. But I am glad that I knew Aran in the 1960s, when it was possible to bring to Inishere a Tibetan friend and hear him say that on those islands, as nowhere else in Europe, he felt at ease.

Artificially created fields on Inishmaan, one of the three Aran Islands. As these islands consist mainly of bare rock the islanders have had to make their fields, using donkey-loads of sand and seaweed, laid in alternate layers. The humus thus created is protected against the rough Atlantic gales by high dry-stone walls which also store the sun's heat and act as a 'thermostat'.

Gaels,
Hurlers
and
Priests

A few years ago I was eavesdropping on the Fishguard-Rosslare car-ferry, as one does when travelling alone. Beside me at the bar stood an elderly Englishman, tall, tweedy, self-confident, all set for a fishing holiday in Connemara. 'We usually spend September in Eire,' he was explaining to his companion. 'Splendid people, really — we have no problems. But keep off religion and politics!' He was all benign condescension, oblivious to the implications of his arid advice — which unfortunately was also good advice. Like so many of his kind, he was caught in a sad vicious circle. Because good manners and prudence alike prompted him to keep off religion and politics, he could have only the most superficial knowledge of the Irish. Therefore, he might indeed unintentionally give offence if he *didn't* keep off those subjects, as most people of his generation were advised to do when travelling in a foreign land. But then, as an Englishman in Ireland was he really a foreigner? Did he think of himself as such when he stepped on to the soil of what he anachronistically described as 'Eire'? (In itself an offensive description of the country, to many Irish.) And did the natives of 'Eire' think of him as a foreigner? Probably not, though a few may have thought of him as an *enemy*. (But only very few; in all opinion polls the English emerge as by far the most popular tourists in the Republic.)

Occasionally one hears a Northern Ireland Unionist, or an English journalist or politician, referring to the Republic of Ireland as a 'foreign country'. Yet the phrase never rings true. It can sound defiant, or self-

Bogland patterned by turf-cutters. Quite often prehistoric boats, weapons and artefacts are found in bogs, which are excellent wood-preservers.

persuading, or insulting: in all cases absurdity tinges the notion. Literally of course it is correct. The Republic of Ireland is a sovereign independent state, technically as 'foreign' to an Englishman as Paraguay or Albania. But history has its own momentum; seven centuries of conquest and re-conquest, rebellion and repression, exploitation and dependence, misunderstanding and emulation, create a relationship that cannot be cancelled out in six decades by constitutional changes. It may be in many ways a stressful and mutually suspicious relationship, like an unhappy marriage. But it exists. One has a similar feeling when travelling to and fro between India and Pakistan; on the non-political plane it is as yet impossible to take seriously their independence of each other.

Jack White has well illustrated this 'marriage': 'I was born a Protestant in Ireland ... I am Irish, in a sense, by choice: both my parents happened to be English, but I have never thought of myself, from the age of fourteen, as anything but an Irishman.'[1] Only someone of British parentage could feel he or she had a choice in this matter. Similarly, thousands of Irish settlers in Britain have chosen to become British in all but family name. For them, the legal and cultural barriers that have to be overcome by other immigrants simply do not exist.

I engaged the tweedy fisherman in conversation and after the second Jameson contrived to break down his conversational inhibitions. Predictably, his awareness of Irish realities was limited to *Daily Telegraph* reports. Yet his affection for the place couldn't be doubted – and *of course* he didn't think of himself as a foreigner in Eire! After the third Jameson it became evident that he regarded Ireland as a lost colony in which he, as an Englishman, retained a certain vague but comforting overlord status – one where the natives, happily, were well-disposed towards their former rulers. His father, too, had fished in Connemara, and his mother had been Anglo-Irish. He recalled the West of Ireland during the 1950s, when you could drive all day without meeting another motor-car and the landscape was undefiled by bungalows and foreign factories – 'all those Japs and whatnot'.

Ireland's aura of remoteness, simplicity and tranquillity has been diminished but not banished by the past quarter century of economic development. Even Northern Ireland still feels tranquil in all but a few trouble-spots, as those visitors who venture over the border are astonished to discover. It would, however, be hard to find a less simple country of four million or so inhabitants. The Northern Irish 'uncer-

Characteristic erosion on the Burren, County Clare. Overleaf: *A classic Connemara landscape near Costelloe, County Galway. Although this land looks so poor, the rich variety of its herbs produces meat greatly valued for its delicate flavour.*

[1] *Minority Report* Gill & Macmillan, 1975

tainty about identity' has become a cliché, and it is both fashionable and true to see it as a major cause of the present political-cum-security problem. Yet those who study the Irish jigsaw-puzzle, in any of the thirty-two counties, soon realize that this uncertainty is common to all the Irish, though its symptoms are much less obvious in the Republic than in the North. Recently the so-called Southern Irish (some of whom live in the northernmost part of the island, in Co. Donegal) have been urged by their more responsible political leaders to help find a solution to the Northern problem by thinking honestly about the question 'What does it mean, in the 1980s, to be Irish?' Thus they are being indirectly encouraged to recognize that the National Identity fashioned for them by the founders of the state is false – and dangerously so.

In 1979 Dr F. S. L. Lyons, a former provost of Trinity College, Dublin, diagnosed cruelly but accurately that we Irish suffer from 'cultural mongrelism.'[1] He made plain the dire consequences of our failure to recognize the Irish jigsaw puzzle for what it is. In his view, there are at least four main interlocking cultures – Gaelic, English, Anglo-Irish and Ulster Protestant, although he also conceded that others could be added. I myself would include 'Dublin Irish', which happens to be my own inherited brand of the various forms of 'Irishness' on offer.

There is at least as much difference between Dublin Irish and Gaelic as between Anglo-Irish and Ulster Protestant. By now true Dubliners are a shrinking minority in a city mainly occupied by 'settlers' from beyond the Pale, but they remain a breed (or cross-breed) apart. In the best book ever written about our capital Brendan Lehane has remarked that 'Dublin was for most of its existence hardly Irish at all.'[2] With this no Dubliner would agree, though it is doubtless an objectively correct assessment. The eighth-century Viking invaders developed whatever primitive village they found on the banks of the Liffey and Dublin remained a foreign stronghold – save for one brief interval in the eleventh century – until 1921. Understandably, therefore, 'Dublin Jackeens' have always been regarded with uneasy hostility by their rural compatriots. The eleventh-century annalists frequently referred to 'the foreigners of Dublin', by which they meant the entire population of the city. And in 1930, when my father was posted to Co. Waterford as librarian, there were angry objections to 'a foreigner from Dublin' being given that 'good job' (salary: £250 *p.a.*). Even today, if you joggle the jigsaw, a psychological Pale appears between Dubliners and 'the rest'. In an odd way, this barrier is felt by some to be even more divisive than

[1]*Culture and Anarchy in Ireland 1890-1930* Clarendon Press, 1979 [2]*Dublin* Time-Life Books, 1978

Autumn landscape near Delphi, County Mayo – a popular angling area – with Ben Gorm in the background. Mayo has always been the poorest of Connaught's five counties, which means the poorest county in Ireland. It is also one of the most beautiful. Delphi owes its somewhat unexpected name to a young Marquess of Sligo, newly back from the Grand Tour.

the barrier between Irish countryfolk and their neighbours, the Anglo-Irish gentry – two groups which for so long have shared so many rural concerns and interests. Although Dublin has been described as 'a pocket-sized capital', its natives, like the Cockneys, are quintessentially urban animals. However, this does not disqualify us from being Irish: it merely makes us a separate piece of the jigsaw. And not a very significant piece, nowadays, when we are so outnumbered by the settlers who have taken over the capital and are mainly responsible for running the country.

No wonder the outsider is baffled when a joggle of the jigsaw tray confronts him with all this. And no wonder the majority of 'insiders' chose to simplify life in their new nation by pretending that only their own piece of the puzzle was real.

Some keen-to-learn foreigners, after weeks spent hopefully groping through Celtic twilights and mists in search of a sympathetic understanding of the Irish, have given up the struggle on finding that the Celtic Revival was initiated not by some true-green Gael, educated under a hedge, but by a true-blue Tory Anglican gentleman from Belfast. Yet the reason for this is simple enough: during the eighteenth and nineteenth centuries the Anglo-Irish were, with few exceptions, the only people who had the necessary education, wealth and leisure for such an enterprise. Also, some of them had foreseen, by the mid-nineteenth century, that one day England would leave them to paddle their own canoe through the rapids of Irish Nationalism, and they reckoned they would be better equipped to negotiate the perils on the way if they took an interest in Irish history and myth and traditions. As early as 1833 Sir Samuel Ferguson (the pioneer scholar from Belfast, then aged twenty-three) described his own class as 'deserted by the Tories, insulted by the Whigs, threatened by the Radicals, hated by the Papists, envied by the Dissenters, plundered in our country seats, robbed in our town houses, driven abroad by violence, called back by humanity, and, after all, told that we are neither English nor Irish, fish nor flesh, but a peddling colony, a forlorn advance guard that must conform to every mutinous movement of the rabble'.[1]

If the modern Irish are cultural mongrels, the nineteenth-century Anglo-Irish were cultural schizophrenics, and some of them have transmitted this disease to their present-day descendants. Ferguson learned Gaelic when that was a most uncommon feat for an Anglo-Irishman, and he truly loved Ireland and its 'rabble' of peasants.

Potato harvest in Connemara, County Galway. From the end of the seventeenth century potatoes became increasingly important in the diet of the poorest Irish peasants, who were mainly concentrated along the west and south-west coasts.

[1]Dublin University Magazine Nov. 1833

But here again the jigsaw shifts; 'peasant' can be a misleading word in the Irish context. As Terence de Vere White reminds us, 'When Cromwell sent the Catholic proprietors across the Shannon to make room for English 'adventurers' and soldiers, some of them stayed behind as tenants and even farm-workers on their own estates.'[1] This explains why nineteenth-century foreign travellers were often disconcerted by encounters with countryfolk who seemed – well, not quite like *peasants* . . . Matthew Arnold, zestfully promoting his 'Down With The Middle-Classes!' crusade, decided: 'Few indeed are the attractions which our middle class can have for the Irish, with their quickness, sentiment, fine manners and indisposition to be pleased with things English . . . A friend of mine who has lately been transferred to the West of Ireland writes to me that he finds with astonishment "how even amidst the most abjectly poverty-stricken cottiers, life appears to be more enjoyed than by a Lancashire factory-hand in receipt of five pounds a week. All the country people here are so full of courtesy and graciousness!" That is just why our civilization has no attraction for them. It has no courtesy and graciousness, it has no enjoyment of life, it has the curse of hardness upon it.'[2]

Not many would now voluntarily read Ferguson, yet he is remembered with gratitude for having discovered, translated and drawn public attention to the long-forgotten sagas and legends of the Gael, many of them pre-Christian. He worked in the Royal Irish Academy and the Ordnance Survey of Ireland with another Anglo-Irishman, the antiquarian and pioneer archaeologist, George Petrie (1790-1886), and with two leading Catholic scholars of the Celtic Revival, John O'Donovan and Eugene O'Curry. These men and their colleagues quarried invaluable raw material for the more widespread cultural-nationalist Gaelic Revival that filled the years between the death of Parnell and the Easter Rising.

While Petrie and Ferguson were busy with their ruins and manuscripts, yet another Anglo-Irishman, Thomas Davis (born 1814), was founding the Young Ireland movement. To him the language revival had a political as well as cultural significance. He warned: 'To lose your native tongue and learn that of an alien is the worst badge of conquest – it is the chain on the soul. To have lost entirely the national language is death; the fetter has worn through. A people without a language of its own is only half a nation.' Davis longed to see a fusion of Ireland's different traditions but his over-emotional romanticism blinded him to

[1]*The Anglo-Irish* Gollancz, 1972 [2]*Irish Essays op.cit.*

Collecting seaweed on the coast of Connemara, for use as a fertilizer. When dry the stick seaweed is removed from the fields.

many of the difficulties involved. He died at the age of thirty-one, yet his influence is felt even today. Unfortunately, it has proved more divisive than uniting. The story of Ireland records many such ironies – not, as is often supposed, because we have remained an unusually fractious race, but because some unforeseeable crisis has again joggled the jigsaw.

The linguistic rescue-bid attempted by Davis, and his successors in the Gaelic League, came too late. By the mid-nineteenth century the average Irish peasant saw the English language not as a chain on the soul but as the only file with which he could hope to cut through the fetters of backwardness and poverty. He was not going to be distracted from that task by any group of well-heeled, starry-eyed Gaelic-cultivating gentry or Dublin intellectuals. Some Gaelic League myth-makers gave their readers heart-rending accounts of cowed Irish children being bullied into learning English in the National Schools. In fact, the majority learned it eagerly, egged on by parents keenly aware of the practical advantages of speaking the conquerors' tongue. Even had they recognized the truth of Davis's 'half a nation' warning they would not have done otherwise. They could not then afford the luxury of nationalism; survival was all. So the bulk of the population willingly exposed themselves to Anglicization while the Celtic Revivalists, the Young Irelanders and the Gaelic Leaguers fought their different kinds of rearguard actions in defence of the national soul.

In 1846 Standish O'Grady was born, and in 1860 Douglas Hyde – the first President of Ireland, at whose funeral I was a seventeen-year-old mourner. These two sons of Protestant clergymen carried on the Ferguson-Davis tradition, with various modifications, leading a movement of brilliant young Trinity College graduates which included T. W. Rolleston and Charles Oldham. O'Grady – described by Lady Gregory as a 'Fenian-Unionist' – gave W. B. Yeats the key to a whole treasure-trove of Gaelic inspiration and was a scornful opponent of Parnellite democratic nationalism. In 1985 his vision of where such nationalism might lead Ireland seems not a million miles off the mark: 'If you wish to see anarchy and civil war, brutal despotisms alternating with bloody lawlessness, or, on the other side, a shabby, sordid Irish Republic, ruled by knavish, corrupt politicians and the ignoble rich, you will travel the way of *egalité*.'[1]

Douglas Hyde became President of the Gaelic League, founded in 1893 by a young Catholic Antrim civil servant, Eoin MacNeill, for 'the Extension of the Movement to Preserve and Spread the Irish Language'.

[1]Quoted by F. S. L. Lyons *Culture and Anarchy in Ireland 1890-1930*

Seaweed collecting off the coast of Donegal.

Hyde urged people not only to learn the Irish language but to wear Irish clothes, play Irish games, listen to Irish music, give their children Irish names, and to boycott English habits, English outlooks, English goods. Thus he unwittingly contributed to that growth of anti-Englishness which many in the new Ireland were to confuse with patriotism. Hyde himself was too civilized ever to oppose *any* culture, in the true meaning of the word, but as the decades passed those frustrations inherent in the Gaelic Revival increasingly found expression in an indiscriminate opposition to things English. It is heart-breaking to look back over that period. Our excellent reasons for feeling anti-English were fewer, in the 1890s, than they had been for generations. Old wounds were healing – until the Gaelic League and its allies ripped off the bandages and exposed them to all the infections of extreme nationalism.

Yeats and Hyde had collaborated on an anthology of Young Ireland poetry but Yeats soon found it necessary to dissociate himself from the Gaelic League, which saw Irish writing primarily as a propaganda weapon and believed that it needed de-Anglicizing. Yeats believed that it needed de-Davisization – a phrase coined by a schoolmate of his, the librarian W. K. Magee. He accepted that Irish literature must for the future be written in English, as a contribution to modern European literature – perhaps indirectly fuelled by ancient Gaelic legends, but not mere regurgitations of them. When he declared that 'literature must take all the responsibility of its power and keep all its freedom' the average Irishman did not know what he was talking about. A failed politician, F. H. O'Donnell, produced a strident pamphlet in 1899 demanding: 'What is the meaning of this rubbish? How is it to help the National cause?' At that time Dublin's nationalist-literary scene was bewildering and troubling for young men like my grandfather, who was torn between loyalty to Hyde's Gaelic Revival vision and admiration for Yeats' already evident genius.

According to Dr Lyons, the 'new nationalism' that emerged during the 1880s 'looked backward with nostalgia to an ancient Irish civilization with its own language, literature and history, and looked forward to the time when the way would be prepared for the re-creation of that civilization by a revolution abolishing not only English sovereignty, but also the more subtle thraldom of English cultural domination'.[1] The consequent compulsion to idealize our past may look silly in retrospect, yet its aim was admirable: to restore Irish self-respect. And the most suc-

Fishing in Lough Erne, Fermanagh. Although fishing is not as popular a sport as in England, it is less expensive to practise.

[1]*Charles Stewart Parnell* Collins, 1977

cessful restoration work was done by a sporting organization which has survived longer, as a powerful force in Irish life, than any other Nationalist Revival group.

The Gaelic Athletic Association is a unique sporting organization. To explain why we must go back a thousand years, to a tenth-century version of an ancient legend telling how the young Celtic hero, Setanta, acquired the name Cu Chulainn (Hound of Chulainn). Arriving late at Chulainn's house for a feast, Setanta was set upon by an enormous hound guarding the entrance. Luckily he had brought his hurley and ball to amuse himself on the journey, and as the hound rushed towards him he drove the ball down its throat. This watchdog had never before failed to repel an intruder and Chulainn was so impressed that he asked Setanta to remain in his household as his guard. This, of course, is but one – though perhaps the best-known – of many references to hurling in the Celtic sagas.

The seed from which hurling grew may be found all over the world; on four continents I have watched small children playing embryonic hurling with curved sticks and a small 'ball' – usually a stone. The Greeks too had the same idea, 2500 years ago. But only in Ireland was the idea developed, and only in the Irish language have the technical terms of a ball-game been used as everyday metaphors for at least a millennium. Hurling is the fastest field-game in the world, and when well played the most thrilling; when badly played it is probably the most dangerous. It consists of two teams of fifteen men each. They use hurleys made of ash plants which are hockey-stick shaped, but with broader, flatter ends. The ball is of leather, and is lighter and slightly smaller than a hockey-ball. The goal is a set of posts like those in rugby or American football; a point is scored when the ball goes over the cross-bar between them, and a goal when the ball goes under the cross-bar past the goal-keeper into the net. One goal equals three points. The ball may be carried on the hurley if a player can find a gap in the defence, and these swift solo runs are among the most exciting moves in the game. To be a good hurler requires uncommon physical and mental skills which are usually acquired as soon as a boy can run, if he grows up in a hurling area. Unfortunately, once a community has lost those skills it seems to be almost impossible to revive them. In 1884, when Michael Cusack founded the GAA in Thurles, Co. Tipperary, hurling was played in only nine or ten counties. Elsewhere, perhaps partly because of a lack of suitable ash-plants, it had been replaced by Gaelic football, first

Hurling match.

mentioned in 1529, and now colloquially known simply as 'gaelic'.

In the early 1880s Ireland's small farmers had at last asserted themselves successfully through the Land League, the first self-propelling mass-movement in Irish history. Now the GAA proved that the rural population, unaided by benevolent Anglo-Irishmen with Gaelic leanings, could also establish and develop a democratic amateur sports association, complete with elected parish club committees and county boards, and could fund it and run it through the efficient hard work of hundreds of voluntary local officials. Even today, 95 per cent of GAA officials are unpaid and the players are among the few genuine amateur sportsmen left in a squalidly commercialized world. The value of the GAA as a morale-booster, during the forty years preceding Independence, is beyond calculation. Incidentally, it also created a sense of 'county identity', as the English-drawn county boundaries had little or no emotional significance until the start of the annual inter-county hurling and football championships.

One of the most momentous decisions made by the founders was to forbid GAA members to play or attend 'foreign' sports – a ban supported by the Association's first patron, Archbishop Croke of Cashel. Having noted that in several areas traditional Irish sports were 'entirely forgotten and unknown', he said: 'And what have we got in their stead? We have got such foreign and fantastic field-sports as lawn tennis, polo, croquet, cricket and the like – very excellent, I believe, and health-giving exercises in their way, still not racy of the soil but rather alien . . . as are, for the most part, the men and women who first imported and still continue to patronize them.'

To us all this sounds nastily xenophobic, yet given the aims of the 'new nationalism' it was understandable. And although 'English cultural domination' was to persist, the GAA has more effectively counteracted its influence, during the past century, than any other organization apart from the Catholic Church. A mass-revival of our language was impossible for economic reasons. A mass-revival of Gaelic art was impossible because the ancient skills – limited at the best of times – had not been handed down, and in any case 'art' is a minority interest. But the ancient athletic skills had been handed down, and among both players and spectators were capable of arousing boundless enthusiasm, loyalty and – most important of all – pride. If the English are profoundly moved, in their quiet way, by the tedious rhythms of cricket, the Irish are rendered ecstatic by the swift artistry of hurling. To the

Inter-parish Gaelic football match.

English, however, cricket is but one strand in the elaborate tapestry of an intact culture; to many Irish, our Gaelic games are a magnificent monument, standing alone as witness to the reality of a more ancient but shattered culture.

In independent Ireland the All-Ireland Finals, held at Croke Park on the first and third Sundays of September, became National Institutions which make the appeal of Cup Finals at Wembley or Test Matches at Lords seem pathetically narrow. In the enclosed and upholstered VIP section of the Hogan stand one sees the President of Ireland and the Taoiseach (the Prime Minister), amidst an array of archbishops, bishops, cabinet ministers, senior civil servants, tycoons, chairmen of state companies – and of course the President of the GAA, who in the eyes of many is scarcely less important than the President of Ireland. If Ireland had an Establishment, that would be it. After the playing of the official political national anthem ('Soldiers Are We'), and the unofficial religious national anthem ('Faith of Our Fathers'), the ball is thrown in by the Archbishop of Cashel who has, as it were, inherited the honour of being patron of the GAA. And then a special mobile cardiac emergency unit goes on the alert because every year the excitement of the Final proves too much for several elderly hearts.

The atmosphere at any major GAA match is unique; there is much more to it than the enjoyable tension normally generated by important team-game contests. Ninety thousand people have attended a Final (a staggering proportion of our tiny population) and one senses that all these thousands are united, beneath the surface rivalry, by their participation in something exclusively 'Irish' – something triumphantly salvaged from the storms of history. The GAA has an authenticity denied to any fringe group of Gaelic idealists, however total their dedication to more rarified manifestations of our native culture.

For generations the GAA has been giving Irishmen, women and children (a big match is often a family outing) regular opportunities for spontaneous mass-affirmations of what they see as a sufficient National Identity. This brings us to the negative aspect of the Association's ethos, which inevitably worked against the creation of an integrated picture out of Ireland's jigsaw pieces. The controversial ban on 'foreign' sports, which eventually gave rise to unpleasant spying on neighbours and punishing of 'culprits', emphasized the gulf between the rural Catholic Irish and their compatriots. It excluded what soon became an extra-ordinarily influential pressure group from the bulk of the urban

Watching the Irish Grand National at Fairyhouse, on Easter Monday. The Curragh, in County Kildare, is the headquarters of Irish horse-racing and the world-famous Irish National Stud at Tully House is one mile from Kildare town. There are over 350 registered studs in the counties of Kildare, Meath and Tipperary. More than 200 race meetings take place annually at thirty courses around the country.

working classes, most of the Catholic middle classes and the entire Protestant population. The GAA has always been firmly linked to the Catholic Church; Catholic hymns are sung before big matches, GAA sports grounds are called after Catholic saints, Catholic ecclesiastics, or Nationalist heroes, preferably of the martyred sort. Pluralism would have been considered a dirty word if any GAA member had ever heard of it. In the Association's vision of a New Ireland there was no welcoming niche for minorities, whether religious, racial or cultural. Not that it advocated any sort of active discrimination; it simply ignored such groups, as though that 25 per cent of the island's population which was so inconveniently neither Catholic nor Nationalist would go away if Gaelic heads were kept in the sand for long enough.

Soon after the GAA's foundation young men proudly bearing hurleys were providing Parnell with a bodyguard at public meetings, and hurlers formed a guard of honour at his funeral. Already the authorities had identified this astonishing new organization with extreme Nationalism, and when the fighting started GAA members were right out in front. In post-Treaty Ireland the Association continued to be identified with 'true patriotism' and the time came when it began to look for its reward as a reliable bastion against 'English cultural domination'. Its mystique was then successfully extended to the political playing field. As a candidate for the Dail (Irish parliament), any well-known hurler or footballer has a built-in advantage over his rivals, although they may be incomparably better qualified to represent a constituency. All Irish political parties quickly learned this trick in the electioneering game. It is still pretty well fool-proof. Owen McCrohan, writing in the *Irish Times* in January 1984, noted disdainfully that 'the illogical tradition by which GAA sportsmen in Ireland are regularly foisted upon the electorate may be a measure of political immaturity but it is, nevertheless, a reality that goes back to the foundations of the State . . . The latest GAA star turned politician is thirty-year-old Jim Denihan, the famed Kerry footballer, now in the Senate. A physical education teacher and the holder of five All-Ireland medals . . . with little to sustain him other than his reputation as a footballer and an assumed appeal to the younger generation, he polled 5,820 first preference votes in the General Election: a tremendous showing for a first-timer with no political pedigree. The implications were not lost on Garret FitzGerald who handed him the Senate job when the time was right.' A week later, the funeral of a TD (MP) was reported: 'As the coffin was taken from the church it was draped in the Tricolour

Above left: *One of Dublin's innumerable bookmakers' offices, known as 'bookies'.*
Above right: *A gambler studying the notice-board before going to the bookie at
Shelbourne Park greyhound racing track. Greyhound breeding is a cottage industry
in Ireland, where many families keep one or two bitches in the hope of producing an
extra-speedy animal which may then be sold for thousands of pounds.*

A game of 'Heads or Tails' being played during Ballinasloe Horse Fair. Stakes rise to £5 or £10. The Irish will bet on almost anything.

At Ballinasloe Horse Fair a tinker's horse shows his paces. Many of these horses are piebald or skewbald.

and a black and white football jersey on top of the coffin marked Mr Cowan's membership of the local GAA club.' But perhaps all this may be considered not so much a measure of political immaturity as a mark of our appreciation of specifically *Irish* heroes. Also, in at least one case a man's athletic achievements greatly enhanced his perceived 'leadership quality'. Our ex-Taoiseach Jack Lynch was among the greatest hurlers of his day, winning six All-Ireland medals. A team mate said of him, 'He could pick a ball off your ear without your feeling it.' This sounds like a line from a Celtic saga, yet all who have seen Mr Lynch play know it to be true. It was our good fortune that he happened to be Taoiseach in 1972, during an awkward phase in Anglo-Irish relations when British troops shot dead thirteen civilians in Derry and a Dublin mob burned the British Embassy in retaliation. At that time the country appreciated being captained by such a cool and dextrous hurler; Mr Lynch took several diplomatic balls off British ears without their feeling it.

During the GAA season a total stranger can walk into any rural or small town pub, order a drink and say without preamble, 'Well, what d'you think?' It is safe to assume that the men at the bar are thinking about only one thing and it would not occur to them that the stranger (if Irish) might be thinking about anything else. In most cases they need no further prompting to embark on a detailed analysis of their own team's chances of success and their opponents' strengths and weaknesses. Or so it was until very recently. Nowadays, if the men at the bar are young they just might be thinking about soccer's World Cup instead.

One cannot imagine Gaelic games ever being supplanted as Ireland's most popular spectator sport. Recently, however, their attendance figures have declined and their 'special' quality has been diluted by the lifting of the ban and a nationwide involvement in televised foreign games. They are also threatened by a deterioration in physical fitness among the mechanized young farmers of today, by the general urbanization of country districts, by the beginnings of hooliganism at big matches and by an increase in foul play, even at All-Ireland levels. This, in part, is sad. Yet the Ireland of the GAA is only one large piece of the jigsaw. Those who long to see the picture completed and stable must therefore look upon the Association's weakening with some relief – as a mark of progress, rather than any sort of defeat.

A remarkable characteristic of all the Gaelic Revival movements (except the most successful athletic one) was their non-sectarianism. In nine-

Modern cemetery of Monasterboice. On a grave in the foreground are plastic flowers under a glass dome, and a wreath of fresh flowers, indicating the anniversary of a death, when many families return to pray at the grave and leave floral decorations.

teenth-century Ireland it was unusual for the gulf between Protestant and Catholic to be bridged at any level of society, as most travellers noted with varying degrees of surprise and disapproval. In the 1820s Lord Mount Cashel requested the government to block the building of 'a Popish bridge' at Youghal. This prompted Thomas Wyse, the Irish Whig MP, to comment: 'Balls, dinners, dances, and dresses, like bridges and hotels, and for aught I know rivers, are divided into Popish or Protestant.' In 1835 the French historian, de Tocqueville, was told by a Protestant barrister in Kilkenny, 'You cannot conceive the distance that holds these two groups apart.' Later he was visited in his Protestant Carlow inn by the head of the local Catholic seminary who observed: 'When they saw me coming in to visit you they were extremely surprised.' The German traveller, Johann Kohl, was bemused in 1844 to discover that there were separate inns and stagecoaches for Catholics and Protestants. In the same year Charles Greville reported: 'Ireland is the only country in the world in which a condition of social and political disorganization prevails, growing out of or closely connected with religious animosities.' This pronouncement revealed a somewhat restricted view of the world, but one sees what Greville meant.

Ireland's Elizabethan conquerors had not been too bothered about spreading the Reformed faith. They were soldiers, not missionaries, and their job was to eradicate Catholicism as a political threat rather than to persuade the Irish that Protestantism washes souls whiter. From then on, there was no hope of detaching the Irish from Catholicism. In Gaelic Ireland the Papacy had never been popular before, but now it became so. 'English' and 'Protestant' were used as interchangeable terms and subsequent conversion efforts, using fair means and foul (mainly foul), were spectacularly unsuccessful.

The 1798 Rebellion had strong sectarian elements in practice (though not in theory) and aroused Protestant fears of eventual 'Popish' domination. A generation later the Catholic Emancipation Act greatly increased those fears – which became near-panic when Daniel O'Connell was seen to be channelling the energies of the newly liberated Catholic masses into agitation for the Repeal of the Union with Great Britain. At that stage the 'Irish Nationalism equals Roman Catholicism' syndrome took root in Protestant minds, long before it had begun to distort Nationalist thinking. And sectarian bitterness was exacerbated by the activities of Irish Anglican Evangelical missionaries who in the 1820s launched a campaign to rescue the peasantry from

Monasterboice, County Louth, is an early monastic settlement famed for its High Crosses. That on the left — Muiredeach's Cross, 17 feet 8 inches — is the most celebrated. Muiredeach is believed to have been an Abbot who ruled 890-923. When new, these crosses were almost certainly painted in many colours. They are not gravestones but served to illustrate biblical stories for the illiterate.

being, as the Protestant Archbishop of Dublin put it, 'blindly enslaved to a supposed infallible ecclesiastical authority'. Within a few years these well-meaning 'Soupers' had zealously distributed 369,868 Bibles and New Testaments, a figure which impressively illustrates their meticulous book-keeping and suggests that they may have been temperamentally as well as theologically out of sympathy with their laid-back would-be converts. During the Famine these evangelists acquired their nick-name by offering soup and meal to the starving, in exchange for allegiance to the Established church. This naturally brought them numerous converts, most of whom promptly returned to the Roman fold when the crisis was over. Even today the Soupers are remembered in rural Ireland with anger and contempt, long after those responsible for appalling physical cruelties have been forgotten.

It has never been necessary to weave propaganda myths about the Irish peasants' immensely courageous resistance to Protestant coercion; that reality needs no embroidering. And it makes nonsense of the Victorians' 'priest-ridden Irish' image. Until the mid-nineteenth century a priest was often the only educated man in a rural community, and so he was forced, sometimes against his inclinations, to become his people's spokesman on social, economic and political affairs; it was this that fostered the 'priest-ridden' image. But the tap-root of modern clerical power in Ireland goes back to the Penal days when Catholics were fiercely persecuted. And the bond then formed between priests and people was strengthened during the struggle for Catholic Emancipation. In 1847 Lord Clarendon wrote to Lord Russell that 'an Irishman loves his religion and the ministers of his church, not so much for their own sake and his own spiritual welfare, as because he is deeply impressed with the idea that they are national. Nor is this to be wondered at if we bear in mind the enormous weight of oppression and civil persecution which a steadfast adherence to their religion has entailed upon the Roman Catholics of Ireland.' De Tocqueville was struck by 'the unbelievable unity between the Irish clergy and the Catholic population' which he attributed to the fact that 'not only are the clergy paid by the people but all the upper classes are Protestants and enemies'. In 1836 the Reverend Baptist Noel, a leading evangelical preacher from London, conceded that 'a persecuted and sympathizing clergy has been the object of almost idolatrous veneration'.

Yet the priest was seen not only – or even primarily – as a national symbol or leader. Among a people by nature deeply religious there was

A weatherbeaten wooden cross on the rocky isle of Skellig Michael. The cross stands between bee-hive cells, which are square inside though round outside; some have tiny wall-cupboards and were probably two-storied, to accommodate a pair of monks.

a sensitive awareness of his sacred character as celebrant of the Mass, hearer of confessions and administrator of the Last Rites. He was 'the Lord's anointed' and after ordination his sacred character could not be diminished by personal defects – greed, laziness, arrogance or whatever – though these might be criticized frankly by his flock. Indeed, the priests' religious status did not prevent the Munster Whiteboy disorders of the 1780s, which were provoked by greedy clergymen – both Protestant *and* Catholic – as well as by landlords who were attempting to replace the poorest of their peasant tenants by additions to their cattle herds. (There was then an increasing demand for Irish cattle because of Britain's population growth and bovine diseases in several continental countries.) Catholic congregations nailed up their chapel doors, told their priests exactly what they thought of them and assaulted a few of the more predatory Men of God. In Connaught, twenty years later, the Thrashers threatened to kill priests who failed to lower their dues, and there is no reason to believe that they were bluffing. None of this had anything to do with Age of Reason anti-clericalism. It was all in the best traditions of our own robust Celtic Christianity, not yet fully extirpated by Roman orthodoxy.

In pre-Famine Ireland regular Sunday Mass attendance was not, as it later became, the criterion of 'a good Catholic'. Many people lived far from the nearest chapel, or lacked adequate clothing in which to present themselves before the altar. Yet diocesan records show that astonishing numbers received weekly Holy Communion, long before the exhortations of Pius IX and Pius X made popular such a frequent taking of the sacrament. De Tocqueville noted: 'The people have a strong and living enthusiasm for religion. "Take our goods but do not touch our beliefs!", this is the cry which echoes a thousand times among the agricultural population of Ireland.'[1] In 1843 James Johnston, an eminent and widely travelled London physician, got the same impression: 'In no country have I observed the *people* more zealous and sincere in their religious devotions than the Catholics of Ireland. If the chapel be full, you will see them on their knees around the doors exposed to the winds and rains.'[2] (Ireland then had six and a half million Catholics – it was the very eve of the Famine – and many chapels were mere shacks.) Kohl echoed this in his *Travels in Ireland* in 1844: 'The Irish are the most genuine Catholics in the world.'

However, the picture was a little different among the 'non-agricultural' population. During the celebrated Education Debate of the 1840s,

Pilgrims near the summit of Croagh Patrick, County Mayo. Ireland's patron saint is said to have fasted on this mountain top for forty days and nights. Every year, on the last Sunday in July, thousands of pilgrims climb the mountain before dawn.

[1]*Journeys to England and Ireland* ed. J. P. Mayer, London, 1958   [2]*A Tour in Ireland* 2 vols, London, 1844

Open-air oratory in a Connemara graveyard.

Two brothers helping their father on the last stage of the Croagh Patrick climb.

the Reverend Paul Cullen, then Rector of the Irish College in Rome, reeled off a long list of able Irishmen who had left the Church as a result, apparently, of studying at Trinity College, Dublin. This evidence that not all Irish Catholics could be trusted to retain the Faith when tempted by 'Modernism' and 'indifferentism' strengthened his argument for segregated education, at all levels. But even segregated education could be a risky business when the medium of instruction was the English language.

By 1841, ten years after the setting up of the National Schools system by the Dublin authorities, 47 per cent of the population over the age of five were literate and most of the country was English-speaking. By 1851, 53 per cent were literate; by 1911 88 per cent. During the same period communications improved rapidly; the railway service progressed from 65 miles of track in 1845 to 2000 miles in 1872 and 3500 in 1914. This gave Ireland one of the world's densest networks and allowed a wide distribution of newspapers and periodicals, whose numbers more than doubled between 1860 and 1914. Such easy access to English-language journalism further eroded Gaelic culture – and more disturbing, from the clerical point of view, it spread new ideas and encouraged independent thinking. This put the Church on full alert and ever since one of its main objectives has been to keep Irish Catholics in a state of intellectual paralysis.

By excluding all 'alien' influences from the educational system it proved easy to control thought in an isolated homogenous society, most of whose members had just emerged from centuries of poverty and backwardness. At this point the 'priest-ridden' label becomes appropriate and it is sad to think how different things might have been. In 1879 Professor Mahaffy of Trinity College, Dublin, whose contempt for things Irish was notorious, admitted: 'The Irish nation, with all its patent faults, is a clever nation; Irish boys are above the average in smartness and versatility. If the system of education were improved, great intellectual results might be expected.'[1] The Catholic Church, as its spokesmen often remind us, made secondary education available to generations of Irish children who could not otherwise have afforded it. But 'great intellectual results' were not desired by the parish priests who ran (and still run) the state primary school system, or by the Christian Brothers and various orders of priests and nuns who staffed Catholic colleges all over the country. Young people trained to think for themselves might have questioned the doctrine of the Immaculate Concep-

Pilgrims saying the Rosary on Croagh Patrick. In Ireland, unlike many continental Catholic countries, the men are as devout as their womenfolk.

[1]*Report to Endowed Schools Commission Dublin University, 1879*

tion (1854), or Pius IX's Syllabus of Errors (1864), or the doctrine of Papal Infallibility proclaimed by the First Vatican Council (1869-70).

All over Europe the nineteenth-century Catholic Church was fighting a rearguard action, and an important part of its action was the strengthening of clerical control over the laity. The autocratic Pius IX encouraged the proliferation of popular devotions such as the cult of the Sacred Heart and the Virgin Mary, while his official decrees repeatedly denounced every manifestation of intellectual originality, political liberalism and scientific progress. In Ireland the Church's stranglehold on education gave it exceptional opportunities to dominate the mass of the people. But the Irish hierarchy was not peculiarly repressive: it merely took its cue from the Vatican and encountered less educated opposition than most other national hierarchies of the period. Its efforts to prevent the emergence of any such opposition were so successful that a French visitor to Dublin, L. Paul-Dubois, could write home in 1907: 'Among the Catholics of Ireland, even among the liberal classes, there are but few to be found who possess any real culture. We find, on the contrary, a certain form of intellectual apathy very widespread, a distaste for mental effort, a certain absence of the critical sense.' Were M. Paul-Dubois to revisit Dublin in 1985, he would not find its mental landscape as greatly changed as its physical appearance.

Yet in fairness to the Irish Catholic Hierarchy we should remember that even at its most benighted it never sank to those depths of ignorant bigotry regularly reached when the English Establishment was commenting on Ireland. Archbishop Paul Cullen was Ireland's first Cardinal and a scholar and theologian of international stature who played an important part in the First Vatican Council of 1870. *The Times* however was not impressed. Listen to its thunder: 'Had Dr Cullen a single idea of his own in his head, did he know an atom more than he does, had he any natural perception of truth, could he write a word of English he would be wholly unfit to have a position of Chief Pastor of Romish Ireland. As it is . . . without one particle of knowledge, even theological, with an understanding exactly on a level with that of his flock . . . he is as convenient a tool of Irish faction as can possibly be found and is the very man to be the Irish religious leader and authority.' Allowances must of course be made for the peculiarly unattractive polemical style cultivated by the Victorians, whatever their theme. But the irrational hatred with which Irish Catholicism was repeatedly attacked from London inevitably effected the development of the 'new nationalism' of the 1880s.

Pilgrims on the summit of Croagh Patrick.

Paul Cullen's many years in Rome, as Rector of the Irish College, had left him very much a *Roman* Catholic as distinct from a *Celtic* Christian. For almost three decades from 1849 he was both literally and meta-phorically the architect of modern Irish Catholicism. He oversaw the building of numerous imposing churches and the re-building of the native religion to Roman specifications. Only at this late date did Irish parishes get their act sufficiently together to build and maintain durable churches. When Pugin viewed the results of the architectural delirium which then seized the hierarchy he was enraged: 'The real Irish ecclesiastical architecture might be revived at considerably less cost than is now actually expended on the construction of monstrosities and the ignorance and apathy of the clergy on this most important point is truly deplorable.'[1]

Archbishop Cullen stripped the Irish Church of most of its remaining Celtic idiosyncracies, including clerical nepotism. He also effectively championed the poor, opposed political violence, restricted the clergy's political activities, refused to attend the Viceroy's Dublin Castle levees and became equally unpopular with his Fenian and Unionist com-patriots. By contemporary standards he was a liberal Catholic who believed in a 'free Church in a free State', despite Pius IX's 1864 Syllabus of Errors which condemned the separation of Church and State as yet another manifestation of the Devil's intervention in modern affairs. When he died in 1878 he left Irish Catholicism more powerful, wealthy, streamlined and conventionally pious than it had ever been before.

The following decades have been described as a period of 'religious revival', though it might be truer to speak of religious narrowing among the laity, accompanied by rampant clerical authoritarianism. By 1914 the Irish Vigilance Association was excoriating 'vile, filthy, immoral matter unfit to be read by Irishmen and women . . . not the product of Irish brains . . . foreign to every aspiration of the clean-minded Celt and most inspired by hatred of the Catholic faith and Christian morality'. This appeared in the *Irish Rosary* magazine, a journal which makes Mrs Whitehouse sound like a hard-porn merchant. The other side of the same coin could be studied in Belfast where the Grand Chaplain of the Orange Order proclaimed: 'The mission of the United Kingdom is to aim at Protestantizing the world. We must have a certain test of men and their conduct. This book is well-written, very clever, very fascinating, but has it testified for Protestantism? This newspaper is ably edited, but does it breathe a Protestant spirit? This lecturer is entertaining . . . but

---

[1] *An Apology for the Revival of Christian Architecture* London, 1843

Many pilgrims climb Croagh Patrick in their bare feet while saying the Rosary.

what does he say for God and the soul, truth and Protestantism?'

Throughout Europe, after the First World War, the climate changed, becoming generally more tolerant on matters of faith and morals. But Ireland remained impervious to this decadence. In the *Catholic Bulletin* for December 1936 we find the following review of the latest Georgette Heyer novel: 'Unlike many notorious writers of our time, Miss Heyer tells a well-defined and clean story. Yet her books are fresh examples of the disadvantage at which Catholic readers stand when they look for an enjoyable light story in English; even in a wholesome writer like Miss Heyer there is a bias that obliges us to read her, as it were, with an eye closed to one colour in her work . . . The whole picture is marred for us, despite the sparkling picture of old Madrid, by the English and anti-Catholic prejudice. If only Miss Heyer's public would allow her to draw the real Philip II in the Alcazar, that sombre and great king, in place of the clammy-handed bigot whom she depicts! With some touches to bring the tale into Catholic focus, what a delightful book we would enjoy!'

Also in the mid-thirties, Cardinal McRory dismissed the writings of Yeats, O'Casey, Synge and the whole Abbey Theatre Group as 'neo-pagan'. He affirmed proudly: 'Irish Catholics do not pay any attention to *them*!' During the same decade, Ireland's leading Catholic newspaper, *The Standard*, announced: 'He who is against his bishop is against Christ.' And in the mid-eighties (in January 1984) a priest preaching to his Sunday congregation in Dungarvan, Co. Waterford, delivered exactly the same message in only slightly more circumlocutory language. At the beginning of the twentieth century clerical authoritarianism was not an exclusively Irish phenomenon; the odd thing about Ireland is that to a unique extent we remain stuck with it even today.

On one issue, however, the Irish Church has consistently failed to keep all its flock under control. Since the eighteenth century Irish bishops and priests, with few exceptions, have been constitutional nationalists opposed to political violence. They condemned the Young Irelanders, the Fenians, the Irish Republican Brotherhood, the old IRA, and since 1970 they have been condemning the new IRA and all its offshoots. Over the years thousands of devout gun-wielding Catholics have been excommunicated, the Church's most awe-inspiring mark of disapproval. But your Irish Catholic Nationalist who believes that only violence can achieve his aims is informed by his conscience that clerical interference may be safely ignored. Even direct Papal interventions are

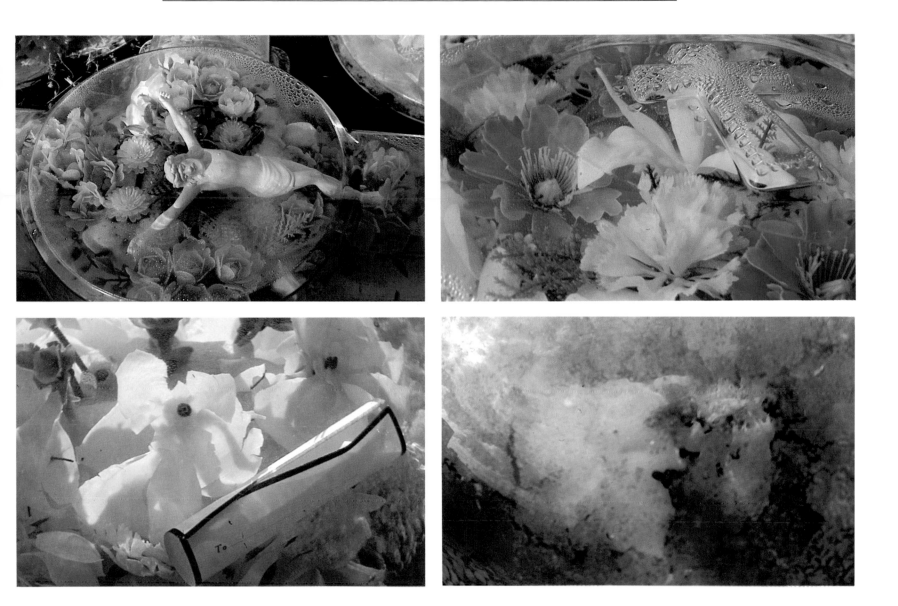

Plastic wreaths at various stages of decay on family graves. Overleaf: Hore Abbey in County Tipperary. Benedictines from Glastonbury settled here at the end of the 12th century as 'reformers' of the Gaelic church. But they seem to have picked up some undesirable Gaelic habits and in 1272 Archbishop David MacCarwill replaced them with Cistercians from Mellifont.

easily explained away. On my desk as I write is a Sinn Fein pamphlet by one Columban na Bahban, published in Dublin in March 1924 and entitled *Ethics of the Irish Revolution*. It briskly disposes of excommunication: 'Reference must be made here to the condemnation of the Fenian organization by Pius IX. There can be no doubt that in this action the Pope was labouring under a misapprehension. The secret societies which justly come under the ban of the Church are those which plot against the Church and the lawful civil authority. Evidently Pius IX was led to believe that the Fenians came under this category and thus he was induced to condemn them. But the Fenians were only out to vindicate the God-given rights of their country: the Church could not condemn a body of men with such noble aims . . .'

Some aspects of Irish life are almost weirdly changeless. When Pope John Paul II visited Ireland in 1979 his impassioned plea for an end to violence in Northern Ireland made no impression whatever on the Republican paramilitaries and their supporters. They too argued that the Pope has been misinformed about the present Irish political situation and would not condemn their actions if he understood it.

Monks at Vespers in Mount Mellery, County Waterford. The numbers of vocations to Ireland's religious orders have been declining during the past 20 years.

Patriots, Politicians and Protestants

At Westminster in the 1980s Northern Irish business is usually dealt with at night, in an almost empty House of Commons; it takes the assassination of an earl, or the shooting of worshippers in church, or a bombed Conservative Party Conference to focus even superficial Parliamentary attention on one of Europe's most intractable and death-dealing problems. But things were very different a century ago. During the 1880s Irish affairs dominated Westminster and John Bull's ability to control his other island was seen internationally as a measure of his confidence and determination. Most Englishmen refused even to consider 'breaking the Union'. In those days of expanding Empire it would have seemed absurd to reflect on the advice of Charles James Fox: 'We ought not to presume to legislate for a nation with whose feelings and affections, wants and interests, opinions and prejudices, we have no sympathy.'

Lord Salisbury condemned Parnell's Nationalist policies as 'fatal to the existence of any civilized society' and put Ireland's religious antagonisms on a par with India's. He warned that Home Rule could lead to Ireland becoming again 'a haven for the enemies of the Empire as in the days of the Wars of the Roses, the Reformation and the Jacobite threat'. In his view 'nations do not change their political nature, except through blood'. The granting of Home Rule 'would require ... a far-reaching and disciplined resolve which is never engendered by mere persuasion, and only comes after conflict and under the pressure of

A 'Big House' in County Waterford that is still flourishing.

military force. To ask the British nation in its present moral and political condition to execute such a transformation would be like making the doctor's cob win the Derby. The forces are not there.'[1] When Gladstone decided that only a fair deal could sooth the Irish, Salisbury continued to advocate coercion. He was obsessed by the need to preserve the pillars of Empire, already threatened by invisible dry-rot, and Home Rule could only weaken them.

The Tories had always been vehement about the necessity to subdue Irish violence without any humanitarian pussy-footing; but they shifted their ground in 1912 when the Ulster Unionists threatened to resist Home Rule by force. Suddenly violence became acceptable – even respectable. The Conservative leader, Bonar Law, announced: 'There are things stronger than parliamentary majorities. I could imagine no lengths of resistance to which Ulster can go in which I should not be prepared to support them.' Nine months later, the Unionist Ulster Volunteers illegally imported from Germany (for the purpose of fighting the British army) 24,600 guns and 3,000,000 rounds of ammunition. Patrick Pearse, watching from Dublin, rejoiced that the Orangemen had brought the gun back into Irish politics; it had been missing from the scene, apart from a few abortive minor uprisings, for over a century. Eighteen months after that the Nationalist Irish Volunteers, mindful of Bonar Law's disdain for parliamentary majorities, imported a more modest 1,000 rifles – made before 1870 and soon to be used during the Easter Week Rising.

By 1914 Ireland's cultural Anglicization seemed to most outside observers irreversible. Nationalist 'extremists' – the Gaelic League, Sinn Fein, the GAA, the Irish Volunteers, the underground Irish Republican Brotherhood – were apparently of little more significance than those who today claim independence for Wales. When war broke out John Redmond, leader of the Irish Parliamentary Party at Westminster, made an emotional speech promising that the Irish Volunteers would willingly fight side by side with the English in the defence of small nations – it being, of course, understood that a decent measure of Home Rule, already in the parliamentary pipeline, would be granted to the small Irish nation after the war. Out of 170,000 Irish Volunteers, only 10,000 refused to fight for England. The fact that so many Irishmen voluntarily joined the British forces during that war – over 50,000 were killed – is proof enough that in 1914 Redmond spoke for a considerable percentage, if not the majority, of his countrymen.

The oak-panelled 270-ft 'Long Room' of the old library in Trinity College Dublin. Designed by Thomas Burgh (the first Irish-trained architect) in 1712, and opened in 1732, it is the largest library in the country.

[1]Robert Taylor *Lord Salisbury* Allen Lane, 1975

The nationalists were appalled by the public's evident approval of this Redmondite promise. Desmond FitzGerald – Father of Garret FitzGerald, the Republic's present Taoiseach – recalled the mood of that time in his autobiography. 'The movement (the Irish Volunteers) on which all our dreams had centred seemed merely to have canalized the martial spirit of the Irish people for the defence of England. Our dream castles toppled about us with a crash. It was brought home to us that the very fever that had possessed us was due to a subconscious awareness that the final end of the Irish nation was at hand. For centuries England had held Ireland materially. But now it seemed that she held her in a new and utterly complete way. Our national identity was obliterated not only politically, but also in our own minds. The Irish people had recognized themselves as part of England.'

Something had to be done about this, and it was. Soon the remaining Volunteers, the true-green Nationalists, were getting Patrick Pearse's message: 'We must accustom ourselves to the thought of arms, to the sight of arms, to the use of arms. We may make mistakes at the beginning and shoot the wrong people; but bloodshed is a cleansing and sanctifying thing and a nation which regards it as the final horror has lost its manhood. There are many things more horrible than bloodshed; and slavery is one of them.' Early in 1916 Pearse was preaching that when war came to Ireland 'we must not flinch when we are passing through that uproar; we must not faint at the sight of blood ... We and our fathers have known the Pax Britannica. To our sons we must bequeath the Peace of the Gael.' Pearse's father, incidentally, was an Englishman who had settled in Dublin; his mother came from a Co. Meath family which had moved to the capital during the Famine.

Whatever the majority of the Irish had thought or felt about the English in 1914, their nationalism was now to be rekindled for them.

The Easter Week Rising began on Monday, 24 April 1916, when Pearse stood on the steps of the General Post Office in the centre of Dublin and proclaimed an Irish Republic with himself as President. Then 687 ill-armed and worse-trained Irishmen took on 6000 British troops, some of whom were also Irishmen. The leaders of the Rising knew that a military victory was impossible (plans for the provision of German aid had miscarried) and that they would almost certainly lose their lives. But they were mainly interested in another sort of victory and they saw their imminent deaths as a worthwhile first step towards the establishment of a thirty-two county independent Irish Republic.

Four of the seven signatories of the Proclamation were writers and three were poets: MacDonagh, Plunkett and Pearse. During lulls in this five-day war, members of the beleaguered GPO garrison discussed writing, philosophy and theology, about which they knew much more than they did about military strategy or tactics. This was a very 'literary' rebellion. Pearse himself never fired a shot throughout Easter Week. For all the fevered mysticism of his speeches and writings, in which he dwelt at length on Ireland's desperate thirst for the blood of Irishmen to be shed to revive the Dark Rose, and so on, he was the sort who would in real life have thought at least twice before squashing a beetle.

As the hour of inevitable defeat approached, a fighting retreat from the GPO was planned. But then Pearse personally witnessed the deaths of three civilians, caught in army fire, and he forgot all about not flinching at the sight of blood. Immediately he insisted on surrendering, against the wishes of most of his fellow-leaders, to avoid further civilian casualties. He was a very mixed-up kid; he would never have made a Provo. It is Ireland's misfortune (and sometimes England's) that today those Irishmen and women who claim to be carrying on his tradition are influenced by his words rather than his deeds. The pen indeed is mightier . . . especially in Ireland.

Whatever one may think about the political judgement, ethical standards or emotional maturity of the leaders of the Rising, it is impossible to deny their courage. Yet Britain could not reasonably be expected to appreciate this quality in April 1916, during one of the darkest hours of the Great War. An Irish rebellion whose leaders had tried to organize German support could only seem like treason, sedition, a foul betrayal, a cowardly stab in the back. But London's reaction proved that 750 years is not long enough for Englishmen to learn what makes Irishmen tick. Sixteen of the leaders were shot between 3 May and 12 May. These included James Connolly, who had to be carried to the execution ground on a stretcher, and then placed in a chair, because he had been too badly wounded to face the firing squad on his feet. To the Irish that didn't seem much like cricket. Within weeks what had so recently looked like the cold cinders of Irish nationalism had burst into flame and the subsequent military repression proved about as effective as hosing a conflagration with petrol.

The Rising was a trivial affair by Great War standards. The dead numbered 132 police and soldiers, 60 rebels and 300-odd civilians. Had the leaders not been executed it is probable that the storm of rebellion would have passed over, like many another before, leaving Ireland again becalmed on the sea of constitutional politics.

What might have happened next is anybody's guess. The thirty-two-county Irish Republic solemnly proclaimed by Pearse on the steps of the GPO, and for which he and his comrades died, existed only in the realms of fantasy, where it has since remained. The Irish Free State, tortuously negotiated during the truce in the Anglo-Irish war by Arthur Griffeth and his colleagues, became the reality in 1922. From that State the present twenty-six county Republic evolved over the years, as one by one all formal links with Britain were broken. But could the Free State reality have been achieved peacefully without the spiritual dynamo of the fantasy to power the political process? Terence de Vere White says, 'It is the sad truth of Ireland's relations with England that she always did best when she was most violent. The ruthlessness of Collins achieved more than the chivalry of all the Irish leaders who endeavoured to treat England as an honourable friend.'[1] This 'sad truth' follows logically from Lord Salisbury's observation about nations not changing their political nature 'except through blood'.

Some form of Home Rule would certainly have been achieved soon after the war; enough Irish blood had been shed for the Empire to ensure that. Moreover, had anti-British passions not been rekindled by the 1916 executions, and by the atrocious behaviour of British forces during the Anglo-Irish war, our island might never have been so decisively partitioned. After 1916, demands for a thirty-two county sovereign Republic made it impossible to reach any compromise acceptable to both Ulster Unionists and Nationalists. This argument is, however, based on an explosively controversial hypothesis. The counter-argument insists that the public gut-reaction to the executions proves how superficial was the Anglicization of the Gaelic psyche; therefore *something* would have provoked violent opposition to any compromise that left Ireland only semi-free – though non-partitioned. Only one thing is beyond dispute. The deliberate propagation by successive Irish governments of an Easter Week cult (with all that that implies, in terms of glorifying violence) is partly responsible for the present dangerous state of the Irish jigsaw puzzle.

The Rising's literary flavour helped those who were eager to stress the heroism of the men who died for Ireland's freedom, while playing down the worth of those who lived for Ireland, and got the show on the road, during the twenties. The Department of Education gave Pearse's

Georgian doorways are a feature of Dublin architecture.

[1] *Kevin O'Higgins* Methuen, 1948

voluminous writings, in both Irish and English, an altogether dis-
proportionate prominence on school syllabuses. When de Valera (a
surviving Easter Week leader) came to power in 1932, Pearse's fantasies
about a *Gaelic* independent Ireland acquired gospel status. The
Department's 'Notes for Teachers' recommended that 'the continuity of
the separatist idea from Tone to Pearse should be stressd. The teaching
of the Irish language is not an end in itself. The aim is broader and more
difficult. It is to restore as far as possible the characteristically Gaelic turn
of mind and way of looking at life . . . Prayers and ordinary salutations
and expressions breathing a high spirituality, a vivid awareness of the
presence of God, and a deep spirit of resignation to His will, are domi-
nant elements in the Gaelic outlook on life.' As Ruth Dudley Edwards
has pointed out in her recent book on Patrick Pearse, 'This doctrine was
almost pure Pearse.'

A powerful minority in the new state had persuaded themselves that
Ireland free would suddenly discover it also wished to be Gaelic. Not so,
however. The seeds of Gaelic Nationalism so lavishly sown over the next
thirty-five years produced only a few healthy plants. Sadly, the main
harvest was a crop of hypocritical posturings as schoolchildren learned
how to feign some knowledge of a language necessary to obtain all
examinations and even minor government posts. Irish is one of the most
difficult European languages – and one of the most beautiful, when
correctly spoken. Therefore, to make it compulsory for the entire
primary school population, as the medium through which all other
subjects had to be learned, was a form of mental cruelty which bred a
detestation of their native tongue in millions of children. Most of them
left school 'illiterate in two languages'. I forget who first used that
phrase, but it explains why so many older Irishmen and women, of
proven intellectual ability, sound like retarded farm-hands when called
upon to speak in public.

The damage done by this official attachment to a lost cause naturally
troubled the Irish National Teachers' Organization, which in 1950 found
the courage to oppose it. Since then, our language policy has gradually
become less insane. It is now conceded (though nobody has actually *said*
so) that Irish can never be revived among any significant section of the
population. This grieves many Irish people, including myself, but since
it is so, one must give thanks that at last we have faced the truth. One of
our most distinguished Gaelic scholars, Arland Usher – yet another
Protestant Anglo-Irishman – was referring to the official language policy

---

[1]*Patrick Pearse* Golancz, 1977

Sunset on Arran Quay, in Dublin, with St Paul's Church reflected in the Liffey. St Paul's (built 1835-42, to the design of Patrick Byrne) was one of the first Catholic churches to be built after Catholic Emancipation, and the intrusion of such a conspicuous Papist edifice on a main thoroughfare infuriated many Irish Protestants. Arran Quay was laid out in the 1680s.

when he observed: 'The futility which dogs every movement in Ireland is the resolute refusal to be realistic.'

That was written in 1945, and forty years later our refusal to be realistic is no less resolute on many other matters. All countries have bouts of manipulating reality to boost public morale or disguise national failings and misdeeds. The results can look like propaganda, or like hypocrisy, or – when it's all got very complicated, as in Ireland – like self-hypnotic myth-making. As the Gaelic League was summoning the ghosts of Celtic heroes to help build a new pure Ireland, the English were complacently admiring their self-portrait of a just, benevolent people altruistically carrying civilization to the less fortunate – and simultaneously their troops were slaughtering East Africans by the thousand to clear the way for a lucrative expansion of Empire. In Ireland the main function of self-deception has always been more innocent in inspiration but equally detrimental to the psychological well-being of the nation. Our leaders struggled to alter reality; and when they failed they refused to admit defeat, forcing on the country a pretence that the alteration had taken place. Hence our mental landscape is still littered with apparently non-biodegradable myths. And these make the sorting out of the jigsaw even more difficult than it would otherwise have been.

Kind people see the Irish refusal to be realistic not as a character-flaw but as an essential defence mechanism which began to operate in the nineteenth century to prevent our becoming so Anglicized that political independence, if gained, would be meaningless. By then – so this charitable argument goes – we were only vaguely aware of our ancient Celtic heritage and brief period of European importance during the Dark Ages. Yet those were historical facts, achievements of which any race might boast, and there was nothing reprehensible about spreading a knowledge of and pride in this glorious past.

True. But the snag was that an awful lot had happened in between – like the Danes, the Normans and the English – making it impossible for us modern Irish genuinely to identify with our illustrious ancestors of a thousand (and more) years ago. For us they have less relevance than the Pharaohs have for the Egyptians of today; at least the Pharaohs are still contributing to the economy of their country through the tourist trade. Yet the Gaelic Revivalists insisted that to bring about a National Renaissance we must be loyal to that meaningless past, from which – if we worked at it hard enough – we should be able to fashion a new de-Anglicized identity. Thus it became a patriotic duty to indulge in

The Custom House, built 1781-91, is generally recognized as one of Dublin's two finest buildings. The other is the Four Courts. Both were designed by the English architect, James Gandon, and both were badly damaged during 'The Troubles' but subsequently restored.

make-believe, and fleeing from reality quickly became a habit. The recent history of Ireland suggests that this course of action now appeals to us as the easiest way to deal with a variety of day-to-day problems.

Some interesting contrasts soon appeared between the Free State's twenty-six counties and the six counties that remained within the United Kingdom. In Northern Ireland the one third Catholic minority was at the bottom of the economic pile and the new Stormont government made no secret of the fact that it intended to keep them there. In the Free State the 5 per cent Protestant minority was on top of the pile, in control of most of the nation's wealth and only rarely discriminated against. (The orgy of mansion-burning that marked 'The Troubles' – over 140 Anglo-Irish country houses were destroyed by IRA Irregulars between January 1922 and April 1923 – was motivated by purely political animosity, and included Catholic targets.) In the Free State's first Senate there were twenty-four non-Roman Catholics, including seven peers, two baronets and a knight, out of a total of sixty Senators; and more than half of these Anglo-Irish representatives had been nominated by William Cosgrave, as leader of the new government. The first President of Ireland was a Protestant, Douglas Hyde; another Protestant President, Erskine Childers, followed in due course. Protestant landowners remained in possession of vast (by Irish standards) estates, and Protestant big businessmen remained in control of their big businesses. Protestant clergymen continued to run their Protestant state-subsidized schools, and special government grants were given to Protestant secondary school children who lived more than thirty miles from the nearest Protestant boarding-school. Isolated cases of anti-Protestant discrimination became loudly debated National Scandals, whereas anti-Catholic discrimination was built into the political and administrative structures of Northern Ireland. The Southern Irish marked the contrast, a trifle smugly, and soon came to pride themselves on their religious tolerance.

Yet as the years passed, and the new nation found its feet, it became plain that both those feet, down to their last little toe-nail, were Catholic. Now as never before Nationalism equalled Catholicism. Consequently Protestants were 'outsiders', though it had become a point of honour to give them a fair deal. The paradox inherent in this attitude was rarely noticed at the time; we were still claiming the 'six counties', and our heroes of Easter Week and the War of Independence had fought and

'Big House' in Connemara burnt during The Troubles.

Sheep-shearing in County Kerry.

A farmer brings home hand-won turf of poor quality in donkey-creels. Turf is still an important fuel in bogland areas of the West but one can no longer say that every Irish farmhouse is pervaded by the sweetish scent of a turf fire. In most regions oil, gas and electricity have replaced hand-won turf. However, Bord na Mona, a State company, produces machine-won turf, compressed into briquettes for use in open fires.

died for a free *unified* Ireland that would have included a million *very* Protestant Protestants – some 25 per cent of the population.

The new State's evolution into a specifically *Catholic* nation was not simply the 'Home Rule is Rome Rule' outcome that had been grimly predicted by Ulster's Unionists; it was at once less sinister and more complicated. Obviously it was the option that could be adopted by the 95 per cent Southern majority with the minimum of effort, merely by turning their backs on the rest of the jigsaw. Partition itself, rather than 'Romish' pressure, created this option. In a united Ireland the presence of one million Protestants would have meant that there was no such option, and having to *think* about the jigsaw would have done a lot to rouse the 3 million Catholics from their intellectual apathy. The Southern Irish Catholic layman is not by nature a bigot or a dictator. He is a live-and-let-live type who, if forced to consider the matter, would never wish to impose 'Rome Rule' on his Protestant fellow-Irishmen.

Analysing our refusal to be realistic about the Northern Irish problem, Conor Cruise O'Brien has written, 'The real answer lies in the peculiar nature of Irish nationalism, as it is actually felt, not as it is rhetorically expressed. The nation is felt to be the Gaelic nation, Catholic by religion.'[1] But if the nation had felt itself to be *truly* Gaelic would it have needed to identify itself so unambiguously with the ultra-ultramontane Irish Catholic Church? A Church which, historically speaking, had only recently taken over the Gaelic piece of the jigsaw, and which Irish Nationalists were able and willing blandly to dismiss when it suited them. As Dr O'Brien admits in the same essay, 'Political parties – especially the most successful of these, Mr de Valera's Fianna Fail – have on occasion rejected advice from the Catholic Hierarchy, and continued to flourish.' It may be that as a new nation we soon recognized the inadequacy of the Gaelic tradition to distinguish us from our nearest neighbour and decided to emphasize our Catholicism instead.

Things might have been different had the new Ireland's Protestant 5 per cent been able gracefully to accept their changed status. But the coming of the twentieth century had seen no narrowing of the sectarian gulf. Professor Arthur Clery, of the Catholic National University in Dublin, recorded in 1915: 'I have only once in my life dined in a Protestant house. I have never drunk afternoon tea in the drawingroom of a member of the late Established Church ...' Yet there were then some 50,000 members of 'the late Established Church' living in Dublin. When Jack White was growing up in Cork during the 1920s, 'We knew

[1] *States of Ireland* Hutchinson, 1972

The 'twelve Bens' in Connemara are cone-shaped quartz mountains grouped in star formation around a 2,400 foot peak. A row of similar mountains stretches from here northwards over the holy mountain, Croagh Patrick, to Donegal's magnificent Errigal.

Bogland near Buncrana, County Donegal.

The root of a tree exposed by turf-cutting.

some Catholics but we never really mixed with them . . . In our modest terrace nearly all the neighbours were Catholics, and we were on perfectly amicable terms with them, but there was no intimacy.'

Throughout the centuries Ireland's Protestants had been chiefly responsible for this lack of intimacy. So it is not surprising that on the whole (there were certain outstanding exceptions) the Anglo-Irish behaved, after the departure of the English, like strangers in their own land. During the crucial early decades of independent Ireland's existence, most of them found it impossible to adjust to being governed by 'Catholic rebels', who more often than not were also 'peasants'. They could not help flinching when they saw the Tricolour where they were used to seeing the Union Jack or heard 'The Soldiers' Song' when they were used to hearing 'God Save the King'. (It has to be admitted that anyone not tone-deaf, regardless of political affiliations, must flinch on hearing 'The Soldiers' Song'.) All this was understandable – perhaps inevitable – yet a tragedy. The new nation desperately needed the Anglo-Irish piece of the jigsaw to provide talents and qualities which the majority lacked through no fault of their own. This was realized at the time; and de Valera himself attempted, behind the scenes, to persuade the 5 per cent to become involved in the national life, as diplomats, civil servants, army officers, academics. But they were deterred by a mixture of diffidence, snobbery, vague fear of 'reprisals' and dogged loyalty to the *ancien régime*. Then, as time passed, so did their opportunities to play a part in public affairs. The Catholic ethos increasingly permeated every aspect of life in the twenty-six counties, and it came to be taken for granted that the Anglo-Irish remained in the background, emasculated by history, looking after their estates or businesses while their country got on as best it could without them.

Stephen Gwynne, the Protestant Irish parliamentarian, summed it all up in 1907: 'England has always distrusted Ireland because of that ingrained and inbred detestation of Catholicism which is to be found in almost every Englishman. There is the true root of the Irish difficulty. The ascendency party in Ireland have always been able to appeal to this prejudice . . . The result has been to breed in Protestant Ireland a feeling towards Catholics like that of the ruling race in countries where there is a colour-bar.' This 'feeling' still dominates Northern Irish life, and may still be found in the Republic if you know how to look for it. But it is inconspicuous now – no more than a crumbling relic of the sad Irish past, like famine walls.

The skyscapes of the flat Midlands are as dramatic in their own way as the landscapes around the coasts.

Getting With It

It is futile, though tempting, to speculate about the sort of society that might have developed in Ireland had there been no conquerors to spur us out of the Middle Ages into the modern world – by reorganizing agriculture, building villages, towns, roads and railways, introducing parliamentary democracy and the English common law and giving us a genuine and scrupulous regard for the incorruptibility of our judicial and administrative systems.

Recently scores of archaic cultures have been almost instantly demolished by the shock of contact with Western technological civilization. Something similar happened, though less abruptly, when the English at last established control of the whole island after four centuries of on-and-off domination. The ease with which they then obliterated our Gaelic culture is a measure of its fragility. Viewing English-Irish relations as part of a global pattern, the English conquest looks inevitable – not just for political/strategic reasons, but because human societies progress (for better or worse) through the domination of the archaic by the more sophisticated.

The Anglo-Irish might have felt less ill-at-ease in the new Ireland if so many of its political leaders had not ignored or denied the benefits of 'the English connection', while simultaneously cherishing them in practice. To those men, who had become emotionally dependent on a myth, history had to be re-cooked to sustain their myth. I have before me a 1920s history textbook which states: 'The people who lived in

New brewery on the Lee near Cork. Lager is becoming more popular among the young.

Ireland in 1169, when the Normans first landed, were chiefly a Celtic race. They were the most highly civilized and the most cultured people in Europe at that time.' The author, Joseph O'Grianna, was a member of Sinn Fein, which had taken as its motto a quotation from Thomas Davis: 'Ye shall know the truth and the truth shall make you free.'

Ireland's poverty, noted by foreigners from the earliest times, is the usual excuse offered by our myth-makers for the Gaels' failure to advance. Clearly this is absurd. Given our climate and soil, and a high level of intelligence, we could obviously, if so inclined, have been as prosperous as England by the year 1600. It makes more sense to look at it the other way round and attribute Irish poverty to a lack of interest in so organizing society that material progress would be possible. In other words, we were poor because we preferred to run our own show instead of joining the rest of Western Europe in its forward march. And that show – making all allowances for the hyperbole of annalists and bards – does seem to have been sanguinary above the average.

'Sinn Fein' means 'ourselves alone' and in 1925 AE (George Russell) warned against this impulse to seek again the medieval isolation of the Gael. He wrote, 'In a few years, if the promised television is perfected, we shall all be gaping while the candidate for the American presidency conducts his whirlwind campaign, not only for the benefit of his countrymen but for the world. The ideal of an Irish culture relying upon its own resources is impossible. The cultural implications of the words Sinn Fein are evil. We are not enough for ourselves; no race is. All learn from each other. We must not be afraid of world thought or world science. They will give vitality to our own nationality. If we shut the door against their entrance we shall perish intellectually, just as if we shut the door against Gaelic we shall perish nationally.'[1]

We did shut the door on world thought (if it could be said ever to have been open) and by 1949 Professor Thomas Bodkin was lamenting, in his *Report on the Arts in Ireland*, 'We have not merely failed to go forward in policies concerning the arts, we have regressed to arrive at a condition of apathy about them in which it has become justifiable to say that no other country of Western Europe cared less, or gave less, for the cultivation of the arts.'

This was scarcely surprising, since we had missed out on Western Europe's exultancy of medieval artistic achievement and had long since lost all contact with our own artistic traditions. Attempts had of course been made, during the Celtic/Gaelic Revival, to stimulate an 'Irish

[1] *Irish Statesman* 17 January 1925

Fox-hunting is an important part of Irish rural life, not confined to the wealthy but enjoyed by all who wish to ride to hounds. There are some eighty-five hunts and each region has its own 'character' from the rider's point of view.

School' in painting and sculpture; but these were as barren as such efforts must always be. Thomas Davis had rather naively published a list of 'Inspiring Subjects from Irish History' and suggested that prizes should be awarded for the best paintings on those themes. Fifty years later Gaelic League optimists were still yearning for 'a truly Irish art' – that is, pictures of Cromwell wading through the blood of Irish patriots at Drogheda, or of St Brigid looking Gaelic and virginal (an unlikely combination, as we have seen). Meanwhile Victorian Ireland had been grievously afflicted by what Jeanne Sheehy has aptly called 'sham-rockery'. The symptoms were round tower, Celtic crosses, harps, wolfhounds, Tara brooches, Ardagh chalices and shamrocks – found together or severally on milk-jugs, davenports, tombstones, table-napkins, pub façades, wine-glasses, the livery of the Lord Mayor of Dublin's coachman, and almost anything else you care to mention.

It is a truism that almost all distinctively Irish expressions of creativity are literary. Anyone who doubts this has only to contemplate the work of such painters as Garret Morphey, Charles Gervas, James Arthur O'Connor and Nicholas Crowley, or of such sculptors as Oliver Sheppard, John Hughes, Jerome Connors. Nowhere is there a hint of any peculiarly *Irish* genius. Yet the introduction to a *1984 Illustrated Diary*, published by the National Gallery of Ireland, sidesteps the reality of this inherent national deficiency. 'There is scarcely no easel painting in Ireland until the second half of the seventeenth century, and the reason for this phenomenon is usually attributed to the political insta-bility of Ireland in preceding centuries. A contributory factor may also be a lack of interest in the visual arts by the soldier-planters granted lands over a wide span of years.' This nonsense is as remarkable for its myth-mongering as for its illiteracy – which incidentally makes one wonder if the modern Irish are losing their verbal skills. The writer has apparently forgotten, or never knew, that apart from a few ecclesiastical ruins virtually every Irish building worth looking at is a legacy from the families of those 'soldier-planters'.

Although I was born only ten years after the signing of the Anglo-Irish Treaty of 1921, and seven years after the ending of the Civil War (in which my parents' families took opposite sides), I grew up never having reason to question the legitimacy, stability or integrity of the nation to which I belonged. That says a lot for the architects of the Free State, who in so brief a time had left such firm foundations, despite attempted

Folk musicians in O'Connor's pub in Doolin, County Clare (top), and a Ballinasloe pub during the horse fair. The Irish have always been musical as well as talkative. The harp was the favourite Gaelic instrument and bards recited their poems to its accompaniment. In the twelfth century it appeared on Irish coins and it is now the emblem of the Irish Republic.

sabotage by de Valera's anti-Treaty Republicans. The latter rejected the compromise solution of a twenty-six county Free State within the British Commonwealth, and our Civil War happened because those who accepted the Treaty were believed to have betrayed the thirty-two county Republic – a Republic which existed only in the imaginations of its supporters. (Could the flight from reality go any further than that?)

However, the present fully independent Republic built on those firm Free State foundations owes a lot to de Valera, who was voted into government a few months after my birth and remained in power until I was sixteen. Having at last brought himself and most of his followers to accept the post-Treaty *status quo*, he skilfully steered Ireland through a series of potentially catastrophic crises, not least of which was the Second World War. Meanwhile he was doing running repairs on the *status quo*. In 1937 he presented the Irish people with a brand-new Constitution containing a hand-picked selection of what he considered the best available raw materials for a distinctive 'National Identity'. With hindsight we can see that that obliquely sectarian Constitution – although it seemed satisfactory enough at the time – disastrously joggled the jigsaw. Indeed, some feel it so badly damaged the pieces we should now abandon all hopes of ever making them interlock.

The stability of the new nation also says a lot for the commonsense of its citizens, who reacted responsibly to responsible leadership. Despite the chaos of the Revolutionary years, for which British fumblings and miscalculations were largely to blame, the Irish endorsed parliamentary democracy and the rule of law at the first available opportunity. There was no seriously destabilizing opposition to the harsh measures deemed necessary by both the Cosgrave and de Valera administrations to control the maverick Republican 'Irregulars' and the Fine Gael 'Blueshirts', an unsavoury thirties group whose ideology has been deliciously described by Jack White as 'a kind of decaffeinated fascism'. Almost overnight, the violent Irish had become as easy to govern as the law-abiding English – in that part of the island where the government was Irish.

Yet the first thirty-five years of independent Ireland's existence were bleak enough. The Irish economy remained in effect a backward section of the British economy and millions of Irish were forced to migrate to Britain – more than had ever previously settled there, the emigrant route to the USA having been blocked in 1922. Thousands of families became pathetically dependent on money regularly sent home from 'across the

Top: *Stone walls in the Burren, County Clare.* Above: *Farmers cutting turf in County Donegal. They cut in May or June and leave the loosely piled sods to dry on the bog for six to eight weeks.*

Shepherd in the Wicklow Mountains.

Bullocks going aboard a ship on Waterford Quay. Many cattle are now exported to Libya and the Middle East.

water'; whatever the history-books might say, or the politicians and priests, England was clearly a place modern Ireland could not do without. This caused less disillusionment than might have been expected. Since the late nineteenth century most Irish people had accepted (without thinking too much about it) that whatever form of Home Rule or independence might eventually be won, there was, and always would be, a 'special relationship' between Ireland and England. The horse-sense of ordinary people everywhere usually keeps them to some extent in touch with reality, even when their leaders are trying hard to prise them away from it.

This movement between the two islands of so many Irish – some returning with English spouses, and children to whom Ireland was simply 'where we go for the holidays' – meant that throughout the twenty-six counties Anglicization was more intense during those decades than ever before. The humiliation of politically independent Ireland's increasing economic and cultural dependence on Britain caused much anguished and embittering disappointment among the country's leaders. Political denunciations of English perfidy and clerical denunciations of English immorality grew louder and shriller. Yet during the Seond World War (always referred to in Ireland as 'The Emergency') Irish neutrality, superbly managed by de Valera, was only relative and frequently bent to Britain's advantage. ('Relative neutrality' is a concept congenial to the Irish.) British airmen who crash-landed in the twenty-six counties were discreetly despatched to their place of origin; German airmen were locked up for the duration of the Emergency. Thousands of Irish citizens fought with the British forces, the government insisted on the removal of all radio transmitters from the German Legation in Dublin, and de Valera's own sympathy obviously lay with the Allies. Yet no one and nothing could shake his determination to preserve Irish neutrality (modified to suit the requirements of a special relationship with one of the combatants), and in this resolve he had at least 97 per cent of the population behind him. The Civil War was temporarily forgotten and the nation united as never before.

There are always a lot of untypical Irish around. Having acknowledged them, it is not too misleading to say that after the war, and throughout the fifties, the typical citizen of the Republic was an extremely conservative farmer or provincial-townsman whose hobbies were attending GAA matches, betting on horses and greyhounds and drinking in the

The village of Allihies on the tip of the Bear peninsula was the centre of copper mining in south-west Cork. At the turn of the century these copper mines were the second most important in Europe, after Cornwall's. Veins of copper-containing quartz twenty miles wide were found in the red sandstone. In 1950 the mines were closed; slag heaps and ruined kilns still mar the landscape.

pub with his cronies while his wife stayed at home tending a considerable quiverful. His grown-up children usually had no choice but to emigrate. He and his family read the *Irish Press* or the *Irish Independent*, depending on their political views, and perhaps a local paper and a pious Catholic weekly. They never missed Sunday Mass and many attended church much more frequently. They would be exceptional if they did not have a few priests and nuns in the family, some working on other continents as missionaries. They were also likely to have relations long settled in the USA. They listened to Radio Eireann if they had a wireless and often cycled to the nearest cinema (rigorously censored) which was probably not very far away. They voted for Fianna Fail or Fine Gael – both conservative parties, in the eyes of the outside world, yet deeply divided because their founders took opposite sides in the Civil War. Their standard of living was low, by Western European criteria, and their expectations were correspondingly modest. It cannot be taken for granted that since affluence reared its unfamiliar and seductive head the average Irish citizen is in every way a happier creature. But he is now much freer to think for himself (if he can be bothered) though many of his fellow-members of the EEC would consider him still pitiably restricted – without, for instance, easy access to contraceptives, or any access to divorce.

Irish society still diverged at many points from the European norm. It was marked by backward farming methods, no economic growth, an annual emigration rate almost as high as the birth-rate (50,000), a prodigious number of unmarried men and women in rural areas, unquestioning subservience to a self-satisfied and rabidly puritanical Church, an educational system distorted by the paranoid official language policy, a sex-obsessed Censorship of Publications Board (no books were banned for their philosophical or ideological content) and a myopic 'anti-partition' lobby which fostered those delusions about 'our six British-occupied counties' from which Britain and Ireland are still suffering.

Reading over that last paragraph I notice four words, chosen without malice aforethought (rabidly, paranoid, obsessed, myopic) which suggest a neurotically introverted society, clinging to its illusions, prejudices and grievances as though together they represented an essential shield against menacing alien contagions. It would probably be too fanciful, after centuries of miscegenation, to see this as the modern version of Gaelic Ireland's aloofness. Or would it? However that

Two eras converge as Kerry farmers contribute to Europe's milk lake.

may be, we went our own way for four decades, becoming steadily more petty, repressed, sanctimonious and unaware both of our own real needs and of life beyond our shores. Conformity was the ideal, in behaviour and thinking. Many of course did not conform; but they had to exercise their originality discreetly, for the herd could be cruel. And Ireland is a very small country.

Then came the sixties, and a spate of sudden changes. In 1957 the Secretary of our Department of Finance, Dr T. K. Whitaker, had observed that 'the growing comment on the absence of a comprehensive and integrated economic programme is tending to deepen the all-prevalent mood of despondency about the country's future'. Soon after Dr Whitaker decided to take unilateral action, and with un-civil-servant-like speed he produced the missing programme. In May 1958 it was published as a Government White Paper, crisply entitled *Economic Development*. Sean Lemass, who had recently succeeded de Velera as Taoiseach, shared Dr Whitaker's view that economic progress should be the nation's first consideration. As a sixteen-year-old Lemass had fought bravely throughout Easter Week, but in pragmatic middle-age he was not a worshipper at 1916 shrines. Unlike de Valera, he saw no point in defending Dark Rosaleen from exploitation by wicked multi-nationals, if that had to mean exporting the nation's youth to Britain. External trading conditions were also favourable to our new policy and by 1970 the Whitaker acorn had become a sturdy young oak. Emigration was down to about 20 per cent of its fifties level, investment had more than doubled, savings were up spectacularly, motorcars were common-place, factories and new housing schemes had mushroomed. And the government was poised to take us into the Common Market.

By the mid-seventies, a tidal wave of wealth had swept over the country, caused by the earthquake of EEC support for Irish farmers. The price of agricultural land went not only through the roof but into outer space; Irish farmers with cash to spare were soon choosing to buy land in England, where it seemed quite cheap. The banks energetically encouraged agricultural borrowing on a massive scale, handing out glossy brochures depicting alluring 'farm improvements' to unsophisticated farmers whose native caution had been undermined by the size of their EEC cheques. Suddenly everyone seemed to have everything – High Tech milking parlors, gigantic agricultural machines that looked as though they had strayed from the Mid-West, battery hen units, pig-production units with infra-red lamps, electric shearers, glamorous

A modernized Donegal cottage.

Lettermullen, one of many coastal isles to the north-west of Galway Bay. Nearby, at Trawbaun and Maumeen, are the remains of two ancient churches.

In Connemara (and elsewhere) many old cabins now serve as animal or tool sheds; few are still used as dwellings. Formerly these cabins were thatched and the roofs held down with weighted ropes; now most roofs are slated.

silage-pits, bizarre feeding contraptions for cattle, new barns, new drainage schemes and at least one if not two motorcars. The frail new bungalows that were replacing solid old farm-houses boasted central heating, wall-to-wall carpets, colour television, deep freezes, spin-dryers, washing-up machines, telephones, food-mixers – every gadget, whether useful or merely trendy, that could be foisted on an undis-criminating public with lots to spend for the first time in its history.

At this stage a few wise old sceptics shook their heads and said it was all too good to be true and too sudden to be good. They were right. In the early eighties land prices and farming profits dropped together, far and fast, while bank interest rates went up to 21 per cent. By January 1984 thousands of farmers, unable to pay their debts and threatend with eviction, had declared war on the banks, who then estimated that at least 11,000 farmers were in 'very serious trouble'. So of course was the rest of the nation. Inflation went up to 23 per cent and our National Debt put us in the Mexico/Poland league. The reasons for this are so complicated that I shall prudently refrain from attempting to explain them. One gathers their explanation would in any case require a volume to itself.

The seventies impression that 'suddenly everyone had everything' was of course quite false. No Irish government has ever been even slightly tinged with genuine socialism and the poor we have still with us – not now starving, or bare-footed, or illiterate, but a great deal poorer than they should be. Pre-Whitaker no one was *rich* rich, but now there are many 'fat cats' at the top of the pile while 20 per cent of our citizens are mainly dependent on social welfare payments.

There is nothing in the Gaelic tradition to nourish socialism. Our pre-conquest Gaelic society was haughtily aristocratic; hereditary serfs were tied to the land and English slaves were regularly imported to do the heaviest work. Gaelic literature is strewn with remarks like 'it irks me that a serf's son should hold converse with me,' and 'It is a strange deed that a commoner's son should slay a king's son,' – and 'It is the end of the world when peasants like these rise up against noble families.' Ireland's post-conquest experiences did little to alter these attitudes. During the Land League agitations of the 1880s, when tenant-farmers were advised to boycott their landlords, they demanded in alarm, 'But then who can we pay the rent to?'

One of the executed 1916 leaders was an ardent socialist: James Connolly, the son of Irish immigrant parents, who learned all about working-class politics in Edinburgh before he moved to Ireland in 1896.

Evening at Maam Cross, Connemara, County Galway. A market regularly takes place here as there are few villages in the area.

But Connolly's suspect ideals were never incorporated into the doctrine of the Easter Week cult. The Irish Catholic Church has always seen socialism, even in its mildest form, as the thin end of a Red wedge. In 1936 our minuscule Labour Party proposed the nationalization of industry and the state control of banking, and were smartly slapped down by the hierarchy. Until very recently there was no pressure on the government even to think about 'social justice', let alone take any action.

Many of the consequences of this head-in-the-sandery are both tragic and frightening. In Dublin's 'deprived inner city area' the youth unemployment rate is 73 per cent, some families still live fourteen to a room (contracepton being sinful) and the gardai (police) dare not patrol the streets. During the first three months of 1983 £200,000 worth of motorcars were hi-jacked and burned by 'inner city' youths. A recent study by the Medico-Social Research Board revealed that 10 per cent in the fifteen- to twenty-four-year-old age group were *heroin* addicts – and among the fifteen- to nineteen-year-old girls 13 per cent – four times as many as in New York's Bedford Stuyvesant black ghetto. The sociologists call this sort of thing 'alienation'. Ireland's thinking young call it 'a bloody disgrace'. As half our rapidly increasing population is under the age of twenty-five there are quite a few thinking young, who now have the full support of certain radical (by Irish standards) priests and nuns. At last socialism is sprouting on Irish soil. But clearly many members of the two main political parties would like to spray it with weed-killer before it threatens to strangle the property speculators, tax evaders and other smart operators who so far have cornered a scandalous share of the goodies made available by economic development.

No less important than the Whitaker-Lemass revolution was the communications revolution of the sixties. During the late fifties the Censorship of Publications Board had been allowed to fall into a state of blessed disrepair. In the course of its notorious thirty-year career it had banned nine Nobel prize-winners and every living Irish author of note; but by 1960 most of those books were readily available, though not every public library was prepared to stock them. Happily, however, pornography is still excluded and few Irish people would wish it to be otherwise. Our liberalism, like our neutrality, is 'relative'.

In 1961 television arrived – state-controlled, by Radio Telefis Eireann (RTE), and unfortunately dependent on advertising for much of its revenue, but not cowed by manic censors. Many consider televison the most important agent of change in modern Ireland. They may be right.

Top: *Horse fair in Dingle, County Kerry, a popular tourist centre.* Above: *Sheep auction at the Mart, Borris, County Carlow. Agriculture remains an important branch of the Republic's economy, producing 19% of the Gross National Product (thirty years ago it was 32%) and employing 21% of all workers and employees (43% thirty years ago).*

Cattle market at the internationally famous Puck Fair in Killorglin, County Kerry. Puck Fair (10-12 August) is a survival of Celtic fertility rites. On the first day a wild billygoat ('Puck') is taken in procession through the decorated streets to the main square where the Queen of the Fair crowns him 'King Puck'. He stays on a fifty-foot rostrum until the end of the Fair. The second day is devoted to livestock trading.

Horse-dealing in Dingle. Street fairs, where individual buyers and sellers bargained, have been replaced almost everywhere by covered Marts in which animals are auctioned. **Overleaf:** *The Horse Fair at Ballinasloe, County Galway, takes place in October and is the largest livestock fair in Ireland; it was once the largest horse-fair in Europe.*

At Puck Fair a prospective buyer tests a cow's teats.

Two people clinching a deal at Ballinasloe Horse Fair. Buyer and seller spit on their hands – an ancient ritual – before the clinching handshake. Here the pipe-smoking seller, and the 'impartial' third party on the left, are tinkers – who now prefer to be called 'travelling people'.

Emancipated young programme planners defiantly dragged sex out of the darkened bedroom into the nation's living-rooms and cheerfully scrambled clear of the repeated avalanches of shock, horror and episcopal condemnation that followed 'outspoken' discussions which elsewhere would have seemed laughably coy. British television was also available in Dublin and along the east coast, and RTE showed many American and British films – its own budget being limited. By the mid-sixties novel influences were seeping into almost every Irish home. Whether or not the benefits of television outweighed the ill-effects is, in Ireland as elsewhere, debatable. But it is certain that important areas of life were transformed by this introduction to non-Irish ways of thinking and behaving.

The benefits of another, earlier revolution gradually became more noticeable during the sixties – in primary and secondary schools, in the media, in pub conversations, in political discussions, in diplomatic negotiations. What is generally known as the 'Irish historiographical revolution' had started quietly in the thirties, led by a Belfast Quaker of Presbyterian stock, Theodore William Moody (1907-84). A fellow-historian, F. X. Martin, summed up Professor Moody's achievement in a radio talk: 'For almost fifty years he has been the single most important individual in the transformation of Irish historical thinking.' In other words, Moody helped the Republic to grow up, not least by encouraging objective analyses of the Easter Week cult. He once said in a lecture, 'However idealistic were the men of 1916, the consequences of their actions in terms of evil results are incalculable. Violence does have its effects but almost invariably these are very damaging.' This Quaker-inspired questioning of the nation's birth-certificate undoubtedly muted our celebrations of the Rising's fiftieth anniversary in 1966. There are not many Quakers in Ireland, yet their good influence has been out of all proportion to their numbers.

At that time cross-border discussions on mundane matters were being discreetly increased, after the historic 1965 meeting in Belfast between the Northern Irish Prime Minister, Terence O'Neill, and the Republic's forward-looking Taoiseach, Sean Lemass. Hope was stirring. Old irrational animosities and all-or-nothing demands were – it seemed – being replaced by a wish for friendly, relaxed North-South co-operation. And we had grown up enough to realize that in such circumstances it would have been crass to continue to elaborate on such a deeply divisive theme as Easter Week.

*Street musicians at the famous Connemara Pony Show, Clifden, County Galway,
held annually in August. Connemara ponies are noted for their hardiness and
intelligence.*

Then, in 1969, Northern Ireland collapsed into violence, demolishing those hopes so recently raised. The O'Neill reforms were judged too slow-moving and hesitant by a one third minority whose patience had worn thin after half a century of remorseless discrimination. In October 1968 Orange extremists opposed to *any* reforms attacked unarmed Civil Rights marchers, and the conflict that developed is still going on.

Sixteen years and more than 2,200 deaths later, most Southern Irish angrily condemn Northern violence, whatever its source, while dodging the reality of our own indirect but potent contribution to it. The ethical waters have been much muddied by Southern double-think. For decades our Department of Education made 'men of violence' school-book heroes while simultaneously our Department of Justice was jailing, hanging and allowing to die on hunger-strike men who had chosen to continue to fight for a free united Ireland. 'Times have changed', we are told, 'since 1916-21. Now we have our own government which has decided not to try to unite the country through violence and has the overwhelming support of the Irish people.' But to counter this logical argument the IRA can and do recall that during Easter Week the overwhelming majority of the Irish people were against 'the Rebels'. As the defeated Volunteers were being led away to jail at the end of the Week, crowds of Dubliners booed them, and threw rotten eggs and vegetables at them – which of course did not worry Pearse. On the eve of his execution he wrote to his mother: 'This is the death I should have asked for if God had given me the choice of all deaths – to die a soldier's death for Ireland and for freedom. We have done right. People will say hard things of us now, but later on they will praise us.'

In 1972, when the Northern conflict was at its bloodiest, Professor Moody said, 'The idea of promoting violence is utterly repugnant to me, a life-long pacifist . . . But I believe that there is good in all men if only one can draw it out; and the worst in men is sometimes a perversion of the best. We Irish, of all people, ought to guard against the delusion that those who arrogate to themselves the right to do atrocious deeds in the name of their countrymen must be as evil as the deeds they commit, direct or inspire.' Those words are amongst the wisest ever written on the Irish problem.

From time to time the British have a little domestic quarrel about the appropriate description for the IRA; most see them as terrorists, a growing minority see them as freedom-fighters. This argument proves how baffling we Irish still are to our nearest neighbours, after 815 years

The River Lee runs through the heart of Cork city.

of close encounters. Both descriptions are of course inaccurate. 'Freedom-fighters' suggests oppressed natives gallantly opposing a colonial power, which is a grotesque distortion of the problem. Yet IRA violence is not identical to – though increasingly it is influenced by – the new-fangled forms of international terrorism that afflict our destabilized world. It is a continuation of Easter Week. As we have seen, the thirty-two county Irish Republic proclaimed by Pearse on Easter Monday 1916 never became a reality. *But the IRA believes that it did and are loyal to it.* They feed themselves on Pearse-type fantasies and are as willing to die for Ireland as any hero of the past. Hence it is both stupid and dangerous to behave as though 'improved security measures' can solve the Irish problem. The British army can never 'beat the terrorists' – for every two they shoot, four recruits will join the IRA.

Only the people of our two islands, acting through their politicians, can solve this problem. And to become capable of doing so they must first somehow break free from the sticky webs of their own inherited myths. This is not the place to consider British or Orange myths. But in the context of Northern Irish violence our own 'resolute refusal to be realistic' appears not as a comic or pathetic Irish weakness but as a menace to ourselves and to others. There remains a large minority of Southern 'patriots', untouched by the Moody revolution, who cannot bring themselves to face the fact that a united Ireland of the Pearse variety is unattainable and must remain so for the forseeable future. These people, while vigorously condemning the present IRA campaign, continue to promote the Easter Week cult. They are apparently unable to see that all the passion it arouses cannot possibly be contained within the approved confines of that cult but must inevitably spill over into violent emulations of its gods. Also, by fostering 'the national aspiration' among the Southern electorate, they – as much as the Orangemen – are maintaining a climate in which it is impossible to discuss any realistic solution. The historiographical revolutionaries still have a long hard battle to fight.

Ireland's fourth revolution of the sixties – which in retrospect may be seen as the most important – was sparked off by the Second Vatican Council. Pope John XXIII's council was designed to bring the Roman Catholic Church up to date, to encourage freedom of the individual conscience and dialogue with 'all men of goodwill', and to abolish the Manichean approach to Marxism. This upheaval affected the whole

A corner shop in Cork city near Shandon Tower.

Roman Catholic world but its repercussions were extra-dramatic in Ireland, where, since the Cullen era, a passive laity had accepted clerical dictates with unparalleled unanimity. Predictably, the Irish hierarchy was reluctant to go with the tide of reform; bishops sulked visibly when there was talk of the 'role of the laity' and 'respecting communists as human beings'. They tried to keep the door bolted against these pernicious ideas, but eventually enough got through to alter Irish life profoundly. Yet it doesn't do to overestimate the impact of Vatican II on Catholic Ireland. By sanctioning dissent it gradually lessened the power of the Church, but there was scope for a lessening of Irish clerical power without its actually becoming weak.

The cumulative effect on the Irish jigsaw puzzle of all our revolutions – economic, media, historiographical, theological – became apparent in 1983, during our mind-boggling Abortion Referendum campaign. I state without fear of contradiction that this pantomime could have taken place in no other country in the world. It was a real-life 'Irish joke' (albeit very black) such as the most inventive ethnic joker could never have devised. We may lack a National Identity but in some respects we are more unique than you would believe possible.

Hearing mention of an Abortion Referendum in Ireland, people beyond our shores naturally assumed that we were debating whether or not to legalize abortion. But not a bit of it. There was never any question of this since most Irish citizens (even the relative liberals) are opposed to 'convenience' abortion; they differ only on the precise circumstances in which abortion is allowable for *bona fide* medical reasons. The subject was not, and had never been, controversial. In 1983 most of us wished abortion to remain illegal, as it had always been. However, it was then *only* illegal; it was not unconstitutional, so at some future date the Dail (Parliament) could have legalized it. This, it was argued might create a situation analagous to that of the death-penalty in Britain, where the majority would probably vote to 'bring back hanging' in referendum, but Parliament has decided otherwise – and so does not, in this instance, reflect the will of the people.

When the referendum was first suggested in 1981, Ireland's realists quickly pointed out that making abortion 'unconstitutional' would not reduce by one the thousands of Irishwomen who annually travel to Britain's abortion clinics. (An estimated 4,300 in 1984 and the figure has been rising steadily during the past decade; it does not include those who give an accommodation address in Britain.) It was calculated that

Dublin flea-market. These markets are important to the many poor families who buy and sell second-hand clothes.

the referendum would cost the country £700,000 – which it did – and an incalculable amount of time and energy. The realists desperately pleaded for that money, time and energy to be spent on changes of another sort; to provide material and emotional support for unmarried pregnant women and girls. They also pointed out that many accidental pregnancies might be avoided by giving adequate sex-instruction in schools, making contraceptives legally available to the unmarried and deleting the anti-divorce Article from our constitution. If there were fewer unwanted pregnancies there would be fewer abortions. And presumably the prevention of abortion was the main concern of those demanding the referendum – yes?

No. Those demanding the referendum close to ignore the fact that thousands of Irish babies are annually aborted 'outside the jurisdiction'. Their main concern was to show the world that *inside* the jurisdiction 'human life is sacred' because we are such a virtuous and truly Christian people. As this point became clear some pessimists decided that Ireland has not, after all, changed much since the Edwardian era, when Synge's plays caused a week of rioting in Dublin; his realistic presentation of Irish peasant life offended the susceptibilities of those who cherished the 'pure-minded Gael' myth. And now, seventy years on, the myth of 'Irish reverence for the sanctity of human life' was being defended with equal fervour by those unable to face the consequences, for Ireland, of the sexual revolution.

One of the many bizarre features of this campaign was its genesis. The existence of a tiny group of very vocal pro-abortion Irish feminists seems to have caused panic among an equally tiny group of lay-people who stood well to the right of Pius IX. This group was funded and egged on by 'Pro-life' organizations in Britain and the USA, and soon a raucous array of pre-Vatican II craw-thumpers had swarmed out of the Irish woodwork to support it. As far as is known, this agitation started independently of the Church authorities, though they were quick to espouse The Cause.

Our 'Pro-lifers', as they came to be offensively known (the inference being that the rest of us were against life), took advantage of a general election campaign to bully both main party leaders into promising to hold a referendum to amend the Constitution so that abortion could never be legalized without the holding of another referendum. Their success was a disquieting example of how a small pressure group, amply funded and well organized, can stampede weak politicians into taking

Top: *Bull Alley Street by St Patrick's Park (on the left). Such 'private enterprise' swings, depending from lamp-posts or trees, are common in Ireland.* Above: *Children at play on a Dublin Street; many poor parents spend extravagantly on toys.*

decisions which they know to be wrong. But least, Garret FitzGerald, as leader of the government, had the moral courage to announce, shortly before polling day, that he himself was going to vote against the ambiguously worded amendment. By then, however, the hypocrisy generated by the debate had reached proportions which can only be described as a collective mental disease.

The Great Abortion Debate convulsed the country for almost two years. It came to dominate newspapers and magazines, wireless and television programmes, political rallies and university debates, the AGMs of various organizations and – of course – the pulpits of each and every Catholic church. Week after week, month after month, the long-suffering public was subjected to arguments about whether or not the referendum should be held – and if so what the wording of the Amendment should be – and, depending on the wording, how one should vote. While our *real* problems became ever more acute these arguments raged – and I mean raged. Throughout the Republic, theologians and spinsters, trade unionists and historians, politicians and nuns, bishops and gynaecologists, philosophers and nurses, G.P.s and housewives, lawyers and feminists, teachers and surgeons, novelists and race-horse breeders – all flung themselves into the fray and verbally tore each other to shreds in a display of Christian convictions recalling the Hundred Years' War. During Pro-life marches and demonstrations small children carried Anti-Abortion placards, while their parents sang hymns and brandished rosary-beads. In convent schools coloured slides of aborted foetuses were shown to the pupils, who were told to urge their parents to vote for the Amendment. At Sunday Masses priests tried to twist their congregations' arms and to confuse them about the issue at stake; all the Pro-lifers wished it to appear that this was a straight vote for or against abortion.

Inevitably the debate widened to include divorce, pre-marital sex, homosexuality, masturbation, incest – and that classic Irish minefield, the relations between the various Christian denominations. Meanwhile the nation's young, from the age of four or five upwards, were sitting in front of their tellies learning more than their parents ever knew about sexual deviations, moral theology and the internal workings of the female form divine. Words that a few years earlier were taboo, and would not have been understood by the majority if used, quickly became common currency. Pre-referendum, the very word abortion was itself considered 'dirty'. But, perversely, this debate made it seem quite

Knock Shrine, County Mayo, which was visited by Pope John Paul II in September 1979. On 21 August 1879 twenty-one peasants, returning from their fields, imagined they saw on the wall of the village church an apparition of the Virgin Mary, St Joseph and St John the Evangelist, and an altar supporting a cross and a lamb. Here we see a marble representation of the vision, by the wall where it appeared.

respectable. From the endless high-powered scientific/theological/ legal/philosophical public discussions, anyone interested could have learned an enormous amount about ovaries, wombs, vaginas, the menstrual cycle, rectal thermometers, sterilization, onanism, vasectomy, ectopic pregnancies, cervical cancer, rape and the difference between semen and spermatozoa. (Orgasms were, I think, avoided in public but only just.) All this should have been riveting stuff for a nation forbidden, until comparatively recently, to read Graham Greene. But it seems we are not given to prurience. Boredom rapidly set in, outside the ranks of the two hyper-active factions running the debate. These might have been defined, at the start, as pro and anti holding the referendum; and then – when the decision to hold it became irrevocable – as pro and anti the various proposed wordings for the Amendment clause; and then – when the wording had finally been determined – as pro and anti supporting the Amendment.

By this stage the debate's most sinister significance had emerged clearly; it was joggling the jigsaw more roughly than anything else had done since the foundation of the State. In Ireland, as elsewhere, Christians differ about the circumstances in which abortions may be considered morally permissible. Yet the Amendment wording finally chosen accurately reflected *Roman Catholic* teaching on abortion and was unacceptable to the other pieces of the jigsaw. Therefore, the adoption of that wording by the Dail had widened the gap between North and South, and between the various pieces of the jigsaw in the Republic. From then on the campaign became a bitterly sectarian conflict, only alleviated by the fact that many liberal Catholics, and ex-Catholics, sided with the Protestant denominations. This development seemed especially tragic because in 1981 Garret FitzGerald had been courageously campaigning for the opposite kind of Constitutional Reform – deletion of the sectarian Articles which block the Republic's evolution towards pluralism.

In a country almost submerged in a sea of troubles – economic, social, political – the public became increasingly exasperated by our politicians' departure to Cloud-Cuckoo-Land. The Republic began to feel like a lunatic asylum as those men devoted more and more of their attention to implementing a remedy for something that did not exist – since abortion was already illegal – while ignoring a massive problem that does exist: all those thousands of Irish babies annually aborted in Britain. On polling day, in September 1983, 47 per cent of the electorate

Children talk to a beggar below an advertisement suggesting his main need.

didn't bother to vote. Some who abstained were registering their contempt for the whole squalid charade. Others had become so confused by the medical, legal and theological niceties of the debate that their consciences had seized up and they didn't know which way to jump. Others would have liked to vote against the Amendment but had been told to vote for it by their priests and so judged it safest to abstain. Others were simply bored rigid by the pantomime – though generally the Irish enjoy exercising their democratic rights. Of those who did vote, two thirds supported Amendment.

During the inevitable media post-mortems, many interpreted the low turn-out as a sign of insufficient opposition to sectarianism. In a healthy Irish society – it was argued – people would have voted massively against the Amendment because of its Roman Catholic bias, thus signalling to the Ulster Protestants that in the 1980s Rome Rules *not* OK. This indeed was how some urban constituencies did vote; but rural constituencies could not be expected to worry about such nuances. Their low turn-out was in its own way encouraging. Many worthy citizens remained convinced to the end of the debate – and are still convinced – that it was all about legalizing abortion. As those were the citizens most exposed to Pro-life propaganda ('A Vote for the Amendment is a Vote for Life!', 'Save the Unborn!', 'Vote for the Amendment!'), their lethargy on polling day carries a message for the Irish Catholic Church.

The Pro-lifers' crusade has boomeranged in various ways, to the delight of their opponents. Pre-crusade, few in Ireland ever considered the rights and wrongs of abortion unless forced to do so by personal misfortune. Now, after two years of thought-provoking controversy, many young Catholics (and not a few of their elders) have modified their implacably anti-abortion views and are prepared to concede that in certain circumstances it may be allowable. Moreover, the routine procedure for obtaining an abortion in Britain has been incidentally publicized as never before. And, although the Amendment has been approved, many experts foresee convoluted legal battles, in the European Court of Human Rights, in opposition to its restrictions. A sleeping dog of some ferocity has been awakened and eventually the 'Pro-lifers' may have cause to wish it had been let lie.

Since the end of the Abortion Debate several cases of cruelty or injustice have shockingly highlighted the hypocrisy of the whole exercise. In one Irish town a fifteen-year-old schoolgirl had a baby, was encouraged by her parents to keep it – and then was told by the Church

Families often run into debt through equipping three or four daughters with outfits like this for their First Holy Communion.

authorities that she could not return to her convent school to sit for those examinations which would have made it easier for her to support herself and her child. In a second Irish town a twenty-eight-year-old unmarried teacher at a convent secondary school had a baby, set up house with its father and was sacked. The father had long been separated from his wife but because divorce is illegal in Ireland he was unable to remarry. In a third Irish town, five months after referendum polling day, another fifteen-year-old schoolgirl was found semi-conscious in a field beside the parish church, having just given birth to a full-term, six-and-a-half pound son. The baby was already dead. His mother died a few hours later in hospital. The principal of the local convent school exclaimed: 'If only she had confided in someone!' But there had been no one, in that virtuous Christian Irish town, with whom she felt she could discuss her pregnancy. All Ireland was shamed by this tragedy. And many asked, 'Where were the Pro-lifers?'

During the past quarter-century Ireland has in practice become a pluralist society, despite the Church's relentless opposition to this development and the State's lack of support for it. This means that our jigsaw puzzle has for the moment been further fragmented. There are now several new pieces – conspicuous additions, yet too amorphous and irregularly overlapping (rather than interlocking) to be easily labelled. The most distressing and obvious of these is simply the Irish share of an international problem, the 'alienated urban young' who have caused a sensational rise in our crime rate within the past decade and made Dublin one of Europe's toughest cities. This novel element in Irish life attracts much media attention and provokes frenzied Holy Joe hand-wringing. Its existence is a tragedy, its future a question mark. Optimists suggest that it may yet do a lot for Ireland if its increasingly obvious needs stimulate a vigorous socialist movement, responsibly led. Pessimists suggest that because Marxist off-shoots of the IRA are politically active among these youngsters we may soon have to cope with widespread organized urban violence.

Another new piece proves that the youth of Ireland has not been dazzled *en masse* by the glitter of permissiveness and affluence. To an astonishing extent – remembering our tradition of thought-numbing education – the intelligent under-thirties generation is being selective as it shapes its own new ethos. And it is learning how to deal kindly with the disapproval of the older generations, who themselves often

Street scene in Cork, the Republic's second largest city. Many Irish streets are strictly functional.

treat this new piece of the jigsaw with more tolerance than might have been expected. Ireland's pluralism is as yet relative and many young people are required by their jobs to maintain a façade of conventional Catholicism. But behind that façade the majority are now free spirits, untroubled by the guilts and shames that in earlier times tormented the few who defied Church teachings. True, some bitterly resent the pressures that make it necessary to maintain a façade, and others are angry because they feel the Irish brand of Catholicism has forced them, against their nature, to live outside a religious framework.

By now it is plain that the Catholic Church in Ireland has missed an important bus, and there won't be another one passing its way. The 'new Catholicism' has much in common with early Celtic Christianity, and the Irish, being temperamentally a deeply religious people, would have found it immensely congenial had they been encouraged to follow it. Instead, many of the young feel they have no alternative but to ditch the Church, with all its works and pomps, in protest against a power-loving clergy still clinging to the wreckage of irrelevant Tridentine Catholicism. Acording to a survey in 1984, summarized in the *Religious Life Reviews*, more than one fifth of Dublin's fifteen-year-olds and more than a third of the seventeen-year-olds no longer attend weekly Mass.

Possibly there is some connection between this discarding of conventional Irish Catholicism and the recent spontaneous upsurge of interest in Gaelic culture – in Irish music and song, and in the Irish language. This phenomenon first became noticeable in the early seventies, soon after the abandonment of the official 'compulsory Irish' educational policy. It is seen by some as a vindication of that policy which, however ill-thought-out, at least kept the language on a life-support machine. Every year more young poets are choosing to write in Irish – not to sustain any myths, or to ingratiate themselves with any political clique, or to whip up any nationalistic fervour, but simply because they have found joy in their own language. Recently over 500 poems in Irish were submitted to the editor of a quarterly literary magazine. Few of these were rubbish and many showed considerable talent. This miniature 'Gaelic Revival' – so valuable because unforced and unfanatical – represents another new piece in the jigsaw, small but significant. Is it possible that the generations to come may see a strengthening Gaelic Revival, in defiance of the video and cable television invasion of our island? Or is that flickering hope just another manifestation of Irish unrealism?

Dusk in the Main Street of Cashel, County Tipperary.

CHAPTER FIVE

Looking
North

In the mid-eighties most Irish people are city-dwellers. Suddenly our society is no longer rural, though urban Irish life has a distinctive flavour derived from its closeness – both in time and space – to the countryside. A growing (though still small) minority of Irish Catholic parents are sending their children to non-Catholic schools to avoid sectarian brainwashing. Many Anglo-Irish parents are sending their children to Irish Protestant schools instead of educating them in England. Thousands of young university graduates, nurses and technical experts are working in oil-rich lands for several years before returning home to marry and settle down. Throughout the Republic, at every level of society, a 'Black Economy' flourishes, though approximately 16 per cent of the working population is officially jobless. Pornographic videos are popular and may even be viewed sometimes in small-town pubs. All these novel developments – some threatening, some encouraging – mean that most of the major pieces of the jigsaw puzzle, as I remember them in the fifties, have already changed beyond recognition. But what of the 'Orange' piece, the Unionists of Northern Ireland? How are they likely to respond to the Republic's multi-faceted revolution?

In May 1984 the New Ireland Forum ended its eleven months' search – by the island's four Nationalist parties, representing 93 per cent of the non-Unionist population of the thirty-two counties – for a new approach to the Orange piece of the jigsaw. The Forum, which met in

Part of Georgian Dublin, showing Fitzwilliam Square and, behind it, the larger Merrion Square. In the top left-hand corner is Leinster House, seat of the Irish Parliament. On both sides of the Liffey, central Dublin is indebted to a 1757 Act of the Irish Parliament which established 'Commissioners for Making Wide and Convenient Streets' – long before any other European city was thinking so positively.

Dublin Castle, invited Unionist politicians to join in its deliberations but they declined the invitations. Only individual Unionists came south, unofficially, to put their point of view.

It is beyond dispute that most Forum members sincerely wished to help solve the Northern Irish problem, yet the Forum's Report was a classic example of our 'resolute refusal to be realistic'. Evidently Nationalist politicians cannot see the kernel of the problem, which is that Unionist politicians are not prepared, under any conceivable circumstances, to discuss with an Irish government possible constitutional changes. They are determined that their piece of the jigsaw is not going to be pushed into a united Irish Republic by any conspiracy – as they would describe it – between London and Dublin.

The Forum Report acknowledged some Southern defects usually denied or concealed by our politicians, but it dodged the Unionists' reaction to the gravest of those defects, the extent to which 'since the foundation of the Free State ... the evidence from first-hand documentary sources certainly bears witness to an inordinate and continual influence by the Catholic Church in matters of public policy'.[1] In January 1985, eight months after the Report's publication, the then newly appointed Archbishop of Dublin, Dr Kevin MacNamara, attempted to influence legislation by denouncing a government proposal to make all non-medical contraceptives available, through chemists, family-planning clinics and hospitals, to anyone over the age of eighteen. (This proposal was designed to replace the Republic's grotesque 1979 law which lifted the total ban on contraceptives, making them available to married people, only on a doctor's prescription.) The celibate Archbishop was outraged. He condemned the new legislation as 'an invitation to self-indulgence and pre-marital sex'. He reproved the politicians for exposing Ireland to 'increased venereal disease, teenage births, illegitimacy and abortion' which he asserted are evident in other countries as a result of readily available contraceptives. He asked, 'If we now decide to sow the wind can we be surprised if we reap the whirlwind?' The Archbishop, it seems, has not been reading the newspapers in his own country during the past decade. The whirlwind has already arrived, and to legalize contraceptives is merely one way of attempting to modify its consequences.

The Irish Catholic hierarchy has its own reasons for preferring the Irish jigsaw puzzle to remain unstable. It could not try to impose Catholic moral standards on a National Assembly in which the representatives

[1]Padraig Hogan *The Crane Bag* Vol. 7, No. 2

Dublin pubs. The better-known 'literary' pubs, associated with James Joyce, Brendan Behan, Patrick Kavanagh and so on, have by now become a little too self-conscious about their role in the tourist's life. The genuine flavour of Dublin's pub sub-culture is to be found in obscure establishments in the poorest areas.

'The Long Hall' pub in Dublin's South Great George's Street, which has kept its
Edwardian aura: plush seats, wood panelled walls, gilt-framed ornamental mirrors,
exuberantly carved mahogany snugs. The Irish take drinking much more seriously
than eating and in many pubs no 'blotting-paper' is available, apart from packets of
crisps or nuts.

174

Left: *Darts is less popular in Ireland than in England but is beginning to attract the young, despite keen competition from pool-tables and a variety of electronic horrors.* Right: *A pub in Dublin's Inner City. In this area unemployment and high prices have drastically reduced the publicans' takings.*

of Northern Irish Protestants held some 25 per cent of the seats.

The Forum Report, while clearly setting out Unionist objections to a united Ireland, refuses to grasp the 'inordinate Catholic influence' nettle. It bases all its suggestions, offers, concessions and arguments on the presupposition that *despite* Unionist objections it makes sense 'to work by peaceful means to achieve Irish unity in agreement'. It consistently evades the fact that most Unionists are not bluffing when they voice as strong an opposition now as their ancestors did a century ago to any form of integration with Ireland's Catholic majority. Instead, the Report lists the 'advantages and attractions' of a united country and stresses the need to promote reconciliation between its two major traditions.

These smooth phrases disguise the fact that to many Southerners the Unionists are, at best, misguided Irish citizens who inexplicably imagine themselves to be British – a delusion wickedly encouraged by Her Majesty's Government – or, at worst, an unwanted gang of land-grabbers who should go back where they came from. The Report refrains from explicitly requesting the withdrawal of the British government's 1973 guarantee that Irish unity can only come about when the majority of Northern Irish vote for it. But the Forum's collective mind clearly favours this sort of pressure from Westminster, though such coercion would hardly create an atmosphere conducive to North-South amity.

The Unionists, too, are dogged by a 'resolute refusal to be realistic'. They cannot adjust, emotionally or intellectually, to the changes wrought by time. They cannot accept as appropriate their natural post-colonial role as just one more piece in a completed thirty-two-county jigsaw. A few years ago Professor Norman Gibson of Coleraine University pointed out in a lecture that their colonist ancestors were 'instruments of British imperial power'. As a result, for over 300 years they have been afraid of their Catholic neighbours whose ancestors were dispossessed by the Plantation of Ulster; and they are still afraid of them. Now there is no British Empire and every other colony has been sorted out, but still the fearful Unionists are swimming against the tide of history. Their insistence on 'remaining British', though they form only two thirds of the population of six of Ireland's thirty-two counties, is the main source of all Northern Ireland's violence. (By now there are of course several other contributory factors, including chronic unemployment and lucrative protection rackets.)

Hard-line Unionism is pandered to, at vast expense, by the British 'guarantee', British subsidies and the presence of British security forces. Yet Northern Ireland remains within the United Kingdom not because Britain wished to retain part of Ireland in 1921 but because the Unionists refused to leave the United Kingdom. Subsequently they ran their own show for sixty years, on utterly non-British lines, practising a degree of religious discrimination that would not be tolerated for one week in any other part of the United Kingdom. When Westminster deprived them of their Stormont government in 1972 they assumed their present position of vetoing any form of alternative government that did not restore their undemocratic powers and un-British way of life. Yet they continue to demand from Britain every sort of military, economic and moral support.

This situation is inherently absurd. It creates an atmosphere permeated by irresponsibility, prejudice and sick fantasies in which it is impossible to solve the problem. London and Dublin are being used as scapegoats. London can be blamed for indirectly fostering Unionist intransigence; Dublin can be blamed for indirectly fostering Nationalist violence. And both those accusations are, to an extent, true. The British 'guarantee' allows free rein to Unionist irrationality, while the Republic's oft-proclaimed wish for unity encourages the gunmen to fight on.

The IRA cannot be beaten without a drastic political change. In December 1983 British soldiers shot two armed Provos aged twenty-one and eighteen. When the present round of Troubles started, those young men were aged six and three. They belonged to the second generation of Green gunmen who have grown up regarding armed resistance to the British presence in Northern Ireland as legitimate, and who can depend on enough support from their community – either given voluntarily or extracted through intimidation – to sustain a guerrilla war indefinitely. The shooting or capturing of individuals is not a victory – 'two terrorists less' – for the security forces. Such incidents merely provoke others to violence; in the Green ghettoes the recklessness of youth is reinforced by the courage of fanaticism. Thus the IRA, though so few in numbers, is unbeatable by any means acceptable to the London and Dublin governments. And each of their atrocities increases the region's tension, bitterness and despair. Yet most Southerners remain shamefully indifferent to the North's tragedy – a fact not always apparent to outsiders because of the ease with which certain politicians can whip up enthusiasm for 'Brits Out!' campaigns. However, 'Brits Out!' and a united

Ireland are two quite different concepts, though often confused by foreigners unfamiliar with the Irish psyche.

The Forum Report acknowledged that North and South have drifted apart since 1921 but failed to analyse the full implications of that drift. One of its most misleading over-simplifications concerned Nationalist attitudes, both North and South of the border, towards unification.

By now the majority of Southerners are ambivalent about Irish unity; in theory they want a completed jigsaw, in practice they would jib at footing the colossal bill. Few have thought seriously about the consequences – social, economic, theological, political, legal – of one and a half million Northerners joining the Republic. Many of those new citizens (both Green and Orange) would be people who despise the Dublin government, many would be fanatical followers of Ian Paisley. And at the best of times Southerners do not look upon Northerners (Orange or Green) as a particularly congenial lot.

Northern Ireland's Catholics are also ambivalent about Irish unity. Those who assume that they unanimously long for it are attempting to deal with a situation that no longer exists. While Nationalist leaders on both sides of the border have remained faithful to the ideal of a united Ireland, at least in their public speeches, several opinion polls taken over the past decade suggest that Northern Catholics have been losing interest in this solution to their problems. In conversation with the moderate 'majority of the minority' one finds little genuine nationalistic fervour – especially among the younger generation. They know that 'unity by consent' is a pipe-dream and are far more realistic in their aspirations than the Southerners, most of whom have never met a Unionist. Of course they think of themselves as 'Irish', but so do many Orangemen – hence the fascination (sometimes morbid) of the Irish jigsaw puzzle. And of course they will and should continue vigorously to demand power-sharing and an end to job-discrimination. Yet sixty years – two generations – is a long time; and by now a significant section of the Nationalist population feels as remote, emotionally, from the Republic as from Britain. Also, the entire Nationalist population is well aware that in a united Ireland their living standards, including medical care and educational and recreational facilities, would quickly deteriorate. Even extremist Green families are now delighted when their sons and daughters are admitted to Oxford or Cambridge; they do not decide to send them instead to breathe the pure Nationalist air of one of the Republic's meagrely subsidized universities. So the apparently never-

Top: *A few of Dublin's scrap-iron merchants still use horse-carts.* Above: *Waiting for the end of the Holy Hour, beside IRA-inspired graffiti.*

A housing estate in Derry, one of Northern Ireland's most resilient and mentally effervescent towns. The City of Derry was given to the citizens of London in 1613 by James I. It was then planted with Protestant settlers who surrounded it with massive walls which have been completely preserved, apart from a 30-ft ditch and three bulwarks – replaced by three 'gates'.

Belfast, the capital of Northern Ireland, is a product of the Industrial Revolution and was hastily built in the nineteenth century. Its factories, docks, warehouses, and long streets of identical terraced workers' houses are unrelieved by trees or grass. But the people – kindly, shrewd, courageous and witty – make up for their city's dreary appearance.

changing Northern situation has changed, in at least one important respect, during the past few decades.

The Forum Report rightly emphasizes that in Northern Ireland 'there are at present no political institutions to which a majority of people of the Nationalist and Unionist traditions can give their common allegiance or even acquiesce in'. It then declares that 'the British and Irish governments must together initiate a process which will permit the establishment and development of common ground between both sections of the community'. Yet none of the three options outlined in the Report has the potential to alter the unhealthy atmosphere of the region. Joint Authority would indeed 'put the two traditions on a basis of equality', but the Green extremists would continue to resent forcefully the British presence, and the Unionists would interpret the Irish presence as Stage One in a Dublin take-over bid approved by London. The strength of Unionist anti-unity feeling has to be encountered personally to be fully appreciated; it constitutes an immovable barrier to any of the Forum's options being adopted. One can sympathize with this feeling, despite the Unionists' irritating obstinacy and paranoid bigotry; they are a brave and honest people and very much out on a limb. It is their misfortune rather than their fault that seventeenth-century fears still dominate their community in the 1980s.

Perhaps the time has come to consider an option first publicly suggested in 1977 but never yet debated in detail by professional politicians of any party: Negotiated Independence. Negotiated Independence for Northern Ireland was closely studied during 1978 by the New Ulster Political Research Group, who in March 1979 published a booklet developing the idea – *Beyond the Religious Divide*. Unfortunately for the fate of this option, the NUPRG is an offshoot of the Loyalist paramilitary Ulster Defence Association. Hence Negotiated Independence has repeatedly been dismissed, by both Nationalists and 'respectable' Unionists, as a screen behind which militant working-class armed thugs are seeking power. Given the UDA's past record, this is understandable. But Northern Ireland can no longer afford to discard any possible solution merely because of its genesis, and the NUPRG's proposal was taken seriously enough for two eminent economists to study its practical feasibility. These were Mr John Simpson of Queen's University, Belfast, and Senator T. K. Whitaker, former Governor of the Central Bank of Ireland and the onlie begetter of the Republic's Economic Development plan of the sixties. Senator Whitaker concluded

Site of demolished terraced houses in Belfast. Within the past few years the Northern Ireland Housing Executive has rebuilt extensively on such sites, providing thousands of cheerful-looking though hardly beautiful homes.

that 'economic viability, without serious diminution of standards, is possible for an Independent Northern Ireland on certain assumptions ... Independence may also have positive aspects of an economically helpful kind, always assuming that most of the majority and minority support it'. Mr Simpson agreed with this view: 'A peaceful Northern Ireland would look very much less dependent on financial support than Northern Ireland is at present.'

Given the blessings of the British and Irish governments, Negotiated Independence would certainly not lead to anarchy and could completely change the atmosphere of Northern Ireland. As *Beyond the Religious Divide* points out, 'It is the only proposal which does not have a victor and a loser. It will encourage the development of a common identity between the two communities, regardless of religion. It offers first-class Ulster citizenship to all of our people; like it or not, the Protestant of Northern Ireland is looked upon as a second-class British citizen in Britain and the Roman Catholic of Northern Ireland as a secod-class Irish citizen in Southern Ireland. It is not the creation of a Protestant-dominated state, nor is it the stepping-stone to a united Ireland. It is an opportunity for peace and stability. It is an opportunity for the Ulster people to get back their dignity.'

If we pause here to scrutinize the Orange piece of the Irish jigsaw puzzle it is seen to be in fact *two* pieces, the Haves and Have-nots – nowadays commonly referred to as 'Unionists' and 'Loyalists', which is an imprecise yet convenient distinction. As sometimes happens with jigsaws, these two similarly coloured pieces have been stuck together for so long that they are generally seen and used as one piece. But the NUPRG Negotiated Independence proposal indicates what could happen when they have at last become unstuck and are lying separate on the tray.

A young Scottish sociologist, Sarah Nelson, has pointed out that 'bewilderment, distaste or outrage seem to have discouraged outsiders from even trying to understand the Loyalists of Ulster. Northern Irish Catholics have attracted far more attention from authors and scholars and have also written more about themselves.'[1] This lack of understanding explains why the worst excesses of Protestant sectarianism are usually attributed to working-class Loyalists – 'the yobbos' as one member of the Alliance Party described them, who in 1974 helped to bring down the power-sharing Executive. Proponents of the 'bloodbath' theory, who foresee Orange and Green yobbos slaughtering each

[1] *Ulster's Uncertain Defenders: Loyalists and the Northern Ireland Conflict* Appletree Press, 1984

Gable-end folk-art is an old Belfast tradition which helps to pass the time for the unemployed and to inform the stranger which ghetto he is in.

Street in a Catholic working-class district of Belfast.

Top: *Funeral of a prison warder murdered by the IRA; on his coffin lies the Union Jack.* Above: *Funeral of a Catholic murdered by a Loyalist paramilitary group.*

other in response to any bold political initiative, can quote the statistics for 1972-3 when more than 200 Catholics, the majority unconnected with any paramilitary organization, were murdered by Loyalists – often in very horrible ways, after prolonged torture. Protestant clergy and their middle-class congregations, and Unionist politicians and their middle-class supporters, do not, after all, murder Catholics. They are well-dressed, well-spoken and apparently more civilized than the inarticulate gun-toting ghetto folk who like strutting around wearing masks and combat-jackets. Therefore, they must be closer than the Loyalists to that area where reconciliation may one day be possible; or so the argument goes. Sadly, few politicians are willing to admit that the middle-classes, both Orange and Green, have a vested interest in preventing the only sort of reconciliation that can ever bring lasting peace to the region – the unity of the Protestant and Catholic working-classes in one strong Socialist party. Since 1921 Unionist politicians have perfected the art of maintaining a respectable law-and-order façade behind which they manipulate Loyalist emotions to ensure that sectarianism is kept sufficiently active to make any talk of working-class unity seem merely naive.

The risks inherent in Negotiated Independence are many and obvious, yet as the Forum Report stresses, 'political action clearly carries less risk than the rapidly growing danger of letting the present situation drift into further chaos'.

Certain facts, some of them not generally appreciated, reinforce the case for Independence.

Firstly, Ireland has never been an independent *united* nation or kingdom. Moreover, the conscious 'apartness' of the successfully planted province of Ulster long antedates the partition of Ireland in 1921. Professor Oliver MacDonagh has written:

> 'The Ulster Protestant sense of territoriality manifested itself remarkably clearly and early in the history of Ireland under the Union. Equally striking was their opponents' recognition – even if it was, presumably, accompanied by a tacit repudiation – of this claim to local supremacy ... There can be no doubt that a set of county limits, quite unmarked physically except on the pages of the map books, was accepted by foe as well as friend as designating some sort of sovereignty. In defiance of familiar and indisputable demographic, geographical and constitutional fact, Ulster, an entity entirely lacking in even

To the sound of brass and pipe bands, members of the Protestant Orange Order march every year on 12 July in their tens of thousands through the towns of Northern Ireland to commemorate the Battle of the Boyne. Women are not admitted to the Orange Order but the eccentric lady on the right of the picture – known as 'Orange Lily' – always marched on 'The Twalfth' for her private amusement.

administrative significance, or religious or cultural homo-
geneity, was regarded as quite separate from the rest of Ireland,
and taken to be a Protestant preserve.'[1]

This development was already irreversible in the mid-nineteenth
century, having been given momentum by Daniel O'Connell's successful campaign for Catholic Emancipation. In his witty biography of the
Liberator, Charles Chenevix Trench notes that to O'Connell the North of
Ireland 'was *terra incognita*; he hardly set foot there, and on one
spectacularly unsuccessful visit narrowly escaped ambush by booking
coach-horses for a certain day and arriving, under a false name in a
coach bristling with blunderbusses, two days earlier'. The 'two nations'
hypothesis perilously raises Nationalist blood pressure, yet 'the Ulster
Protestant sense of territoriality', whether or not one thinks of it as
'Orange nationalism', is an undeniable fact of Irish life.

Secondly, as a group Northern Ireland's Protestants dislike and
distrust the English, despite their determination to remain British.
Below the sectarian/political animosities they are much more at ease
with their Catholic fellow-Northerners. Most of them would resent,
initially, Britain's desertion of their 'cause'; but the hurt inflicted on
them by ejection from the United Kingdom would be counterbalanced
by the relief of knowing that under Negotiated Independence their
piece of the jigsaw could never be painted Green. At present, as the
Forum Report states, 'There is fear, insecurity, confusion and uncertainty about the future in the Unionist section of the community'; and
this uncertainty contributes hugely to the unhealthy atmosphere.

Thirdly, as a group Northern Ireland's Catholics, despite their
determination to remain Irish, regard Southerners as another breed and
are much more at ease with their Protestant fellow-Northerners. The
Republic's desertion of their 'cause' would be compensated for by the
final departure of the British, an end to discrimination and a just share in
the government of the new state. In the eighties the Nationalists' desire
for a United Ireland is very much weaker than the Unionists' fear of a
United Ireland. Skillful IRA propaganda has tended to obscure this fact.

Fourthly, as a group the British see all the Northern Irish as primarily
Irish and incomprehensible, and far more trouble than they're worth.
Independence would arouse none of the guilt that would certainly be
felt by many Tories if the region were coerced into the Republic.

Finally, south of the Irish border Independence would be equally

[1]Oliver MacDonagh *States of Mind: A Study of Anglo-Irish Conflict 1780-1980* Allen & Unwin

Belfast city centre showing in the background 'Samson' and 'Goliath' – the Harland & Wolff shipbuilding cranes.

Provisional Sinn Fein is the political wing of the IRA, and in the 1985 local elections won 59 seats out of 566.

Street scene in West Belfast. The 'H blocks' refer punningly to the prison in which ten Republican hunger-strikers died in 1981.

unlikely to provoke widespread dissension. The 'Brits Out!' goal would have been scored at no cost in cash or inconvenience to the Republic. As Dr Whitaker has noted, 'There would be no need for Article Two [of the Irish Constitution], with two Irish governments between them enjoying sovereignty over "the whole island of Ireland" . . . Article Three, with its unrealistic and provocative claim that the Dublin Government is entitled to rule Northern Ireland, would be an embarrassing anachronism which we would be in haste to bury and forget.'

Independence for Northern Ireland would change the emotional climate radically. The inherent unreality of the present situation would be banished – a situation where Britain is supporting, ostensibly in the name of democracy, an obsessionally undemocratic local majority which insists on permanently excluding one third of the population from participation in government, and where the Republic is claiming the right to rule over a territory where its authority is unacceptable to the majority of its citizens. The removal of both those absurdities would confront the Northern Irish with a new set of positive challenges. As things are, their challenges are negative – how to avoid a Dublin take-over, or how to avoid being forever discriminated against. In such an atmosphere, normal politics are impossible. Fear, uncertainty and distrust prevail. Sectarian bitterness, unemployment and despair increase.

The citizens of an Independent Northern Ireland would of course have to face fresh problems – and some sinister mutations of old ones. Looking at them as they are now, frozen in attitudes which prevent them from contributing rationally to political progress, it may seem that they could never overcome the obstacles to Independence. But in the new state they would not be as they are now. As climates change, so do the organisms dependent on them.

A member of the moderate Alliance Party, Gerry O'Grady, wrote in the *Irish Times* on 18 October 1984, 'The polarization widespread in Northern Ireland can be attributed largely to the cynical exploitation of ancient fears and prejudices by the old breed of "Orange" and "Green" politicians, whose respective philosophies are based, and depend for survival, on the concept of community division.' The most important single effect of Independence would be the abolition of those 'philosophies'. The Northern Irish would find themselves in a whole new world, compelled by the instinct of self-preservation to abandon the cultivation of sectarian division and concentrate instead on fostering that unity without which their new state must fall apart. Freed of the

In certain areas of West Belfast unemployment reaches 60 per cent and the residents have ample time to create elaborate graffiti.

destructive pulls of the London and Dublin magnets, the two communities would soon find their interests naturally converging. They would only have Northern Ireland to be loyal to and the long years of resenting each other's loyalty to the Union Jack or the Tricolour would be over.

There are, naturally, many objections to an Independent Northern Ireland (some overlapping, some mutually contradictory):

(1) The majority of Northern Irish, whether Orange or Green, do not want it.
(2) The Protestant paramilitaries would slaughter the Catholics.
(3) The Catholic paramilitaries would slaughter the Protestants.
(4) The Unionists would oppress the Nationalists as never before; deprived of British support, they would become even more paranoid, defensive and introverted, both in relation to the majority on the island of Ireland and to the influence, within Northern Ireland, of the Catholic hierarchy.
(5) The Provos, deprived of the degree of local support to which they are accustomed, would concentrate all their energies on destabilizing the Republic.
(6) The unemployed youth of both communities, already hostile to authority, would run amok, while the armed protection-racketeers now flourishing in both ghettoes would take over their respective areas; gang-warfare would soon become endemic and the country would deteriorate into a banana-republic unable to afford bananas.
(7) The new state, given its history of sectarian mistrust, could not possibly provide effective security forces from within its own population.
(8) NATO would not permit the establishment of an Independent Northern Ireland.

It is true that now most Northern Irish are anti-Independence, partly because the risks and disadvantages are more immediately obvious than the benefits and advantages. If Independence were widely debated and analysed as a genuine possible option, many more would certainly favour it, though probably not a majority of this decade's electorate. Thus 'lack of consent' is often used to kill any detailed discussion of the idea. It seems people have forgotten that after the 1921 Treaty had been signed Lloyd George told the House of Commons that, if Northern Ireland insisted on remaining part of the United Kingdom, the counties of Tyrone and Fermanagh would have to go to the Free State: 'The

Children of the Short Strand, Belfast. Victims of a society where Propaganda Rules, OK?

majority in these counties prefer to be with their Southern neighbours. What does this mean? If Ulster is to remain a separate community, you can only by means of coercion keep them there, and although I am against the coercion of Ulster, I do not believe in Ulster coercing other units' (*Hansard*, 14 December 1921). Given the lack of democracy required to set up the Province, why jib at another bout of undemocratic coercion to sort out the murderously chaotic mess that it has become? In clearing up other post-colonial messes, British governments have proved capable (e.g. in Kenya and Zimbabwe) of ignoring the will of British citizens whose interests conflicted with a new British policy. A torturing awareness of this potential for 'treachery' explains Unionist insecurity since the abolition of Stormont.

Objections 2 and 3 – that one or other of the paramilitary groups would go on a rampage – assume that Northern Ireland's gunmen are far more numerous than is the case, and that their attitudes would remain unchanged in the new state. Ulick O'Connor dealt succinctly with this aspect of Independence in his written submission to the Forum:

> 'The two paramilitary bodies ... have a number of effective leaders. If they declared their allegiance to the new State they could be absorbed into a new security force. No one knows better how to deal with recalcitrant members of their forces than the guerrilla leaders themselves. They have had to keep discipline in the field. In peacetime they will know who are the psychopaths and who can be employed usefully in working with the State ... What is important is that there *is* a growing grassroots acceptance of the idea of a shared community.'[1]

Objection 4 – that the ex-Unionists would oppress the ex-Nationalists as never before – would be valid only if the foundations of the new state were shaky. Given sound foundations, carefully laid by legal experts, institutionalized discrimination against the minority would be impossible. This Bill of Rights should enable Catholics to live happily enough with personal, as distinct from institutionalized, bigotry – they have after all had three centuries of practice. And the gradual waning of bigotry would be inevitable, in an atmosphere that no longer encouraged an obsessional focusing on religious differences as symbols of conflicting political allegiances.

Objection 5 – the possible transfer of the Green gunmen's campaign to the Republic – overlooks the fact that their *raison d'être* would have

---

[1] *The Irish Times*, 18 April 1984

A new Republican mural on the Falls, West Belfast. Easter Week 1916 seems closer to many of the citizens of Belfast than to the Dubliners of today.

vanished when 'the Brits' left Northern Ireland. Those Green para-militaries who are more Red than Green might continue to work for the destabilization of both Irish states, but the £100 million now being spent annually by the Dublin government to help control Northern Ireland's violence could be deflected, post-Independence, to dealing with whatever new threat emerged south of the border.

Objection 6 – the risk of a law-and-order breakdown – must be taken more seriously. There is enormous potential for gang-warfare in an area where unemployment figures are brutally high and protection-racketeering has become an almost respectable profession. But here again the changed atmosphere would help. The need to unite against the hardened criminals of both communities, and to run effective rehabilitation programmes for the tragically purposeless young, would serve as a powerful antidote to sectarianism at the local level. Events since 1968 have convinced many outsiders that the Northern Irish are abnormally violent and lawless, yet before that date Northern Ireland had the lowest crime rate in Western Europe.

Objection 7 – the inability of the new state to provide its own security forces – has been given added substance during the past few years by the uncontrolled misbehaviour of certain members of the Ulster Defence Regiment and the Royal Ulster Constabulary. However, it overlooks the fact that in an Independent Northern Ireland the police force could not be seen by any section of the population as 'agents of an occupying power'. Nevertheless, for some years – perhaps for a whole generation – it would probably be necessary to import neutral security forces, either from EEC countries or from the UN.

Objection 8 – that NATO would not permit the establishment of an Independent Northern Ireland – may well be of more significance than all the rest combined. During the late seventies some of NATO's more innovative minds devised a strategy for a 'limited' war which might be fought and (theoretically) won in Europe. This concept gives Northern Ireland's existing military communications links a new importance and provides a strong motive for expanding them all over the country. In November 1981, at a 'Researching State Structures' conference at University College, London, a paper on *NATO Requirements in Ireland* listed three ways in which Irish non-neutrality could be useful. Firstly, radar cover of the Atlantic. Secondly, forward bases for US rapid re-inforcement units to be flown to join NATO's ground troops in Europe. Thirdly, UHF radio communications into the Atlantic. Radio relay

The city of Derry taken from the Bogside cemetery with the Irish tricolour flying in defiance of the law.

stations on Ireland's west coast would improve Atlantic UHF reception by a few hundred miles – an apparently trivial distance in this supersonic age, but at present some US aircraft have only UHF radio, which is limited in range by the earth's curve because it works through line-of-sight signals.

Eight months before that London conference, in March 1981, our then Taoiseach (Prime Minister) Charles Haughey had informed the Dail that a political solution for Northern Ireland might lead to the Republic's 'long-held policy of neutrality' being altered. There is of course an amount of circumstantial evidence to suggest that it has already been altered, behind the electorate's collective back. When the Irish government accepted funding from the EEC and the World Bank for a five-year telecommunications development plan, estimated in 1978 to cost £800 million, it was presumably realized by Irish politicians, civil servants and military chiefs that this plan would incorporate Ireland into NATO's communications network, thus exposing the Republic to direct attacks in wartime. (The government in its wisdom may have reckoned that this would be a good thing, killing the Irish quickly instead of leaving them to endure the gruesome long-term effects of Europe's 'limited' war.)

EEC and World Bank funding for such projects is always suspect. An American journal has explained how the system works: 'The EEC's special fund for depressed areas offers a fortuitous international mechanism through which American help can be channelled. Its use would avoid the politically difficult task of seeking Congressional appropriations for either England or Ireland. There is ample precedent for America's participation in a consortium with organizations such as the EEC. Similar programmes through the World Bank or the United Nations development programmes have often been preferred methods of involvement in overseas projects.'[1]

Dr William FitzGerald, author of *Irish Unification and NATO*, has noted:

'Successive British governments have thrown a smokescreen over the fundamental and wholly legitimate British and NATO need to retain Northern Ireland in the defence system and to prevent the province from being incorporated into a neutral 32-county Ireland ... In this Britain has the full backing of any US Administration ... For peaceful success in the ending of

[1] *Foreign Policy* No. 37, Winter 1879/80.

The Glens of Antrim, half an hour's drive from Belfast. Northern Ireland's urban squalor is compensated for by some of the loveliest landscapes on the island.

partition we *must* gain the support of the Conservatives and the Defence Departments, and we cannot have that while we project an intention of taking Northern Ireland out of the British defence system and into a neutral state. By our neutrality we present Britain with an insoluble dilemma; with a demand to which a Conservative administration *cannot* accede.'[1]

Dr William FitzGerald believes that 'Defence equals Prevention' and argues vigorously for a United Ireland in NATO. In the event of nuclear war, our being officially in or out of that organization would make no difference from a practical (survival) point of view. On that level the issue is not worth debating. Yet from an ethical point of view it is becoming increasingly important to a growing number of Irish citizens; and from an emotional point of view neutrality has been extremely important, since the foundation of the state, to most of the population. Thus there are two insurmountable barriers to 'a United Ireland in NATO' – Unionist resistance to any form of political association with the South, and Southern resistance to any form of military alliance that *could be seen to violate* our neutrality.

This is not the place to discuss the future of NATO itself, but for the purpose of our jigsaw-game we have to accept that nothing will be allowed to hamper the functioning of NATO's communications facilities in Northern Ireland. These must remain intact and operative until the NATO machine has either been used (in which case few of us will be around to have problems) or dismantled. This NATO factor is perhaps the main reason why Independence has never been seriously considered. A period of destabilization after Independence could seriously threaten its installations, and make it harder to maintain present links with the Republic.

Ironically the Independence option, unlike any other, could let Britain off the hook described by Dr William FitzGerald. The NATO/Northern Ireland link need not continue 'to present Britain with an insoluble dilemma' because of the Republic's neutrality. An Independent Northern Ireland, carefully constructed on solid foundations, could remain within NATO; and the Republic's so-called neutrality would be no more of an irritant to NATO, post-Independence, than it is now. In the new state non-British NATO personnel could take over whatever tasks are now done by the British forces in their role as NATO forces.

Mizen Head, County Cork. A century ago this was one of the most primitive parts of Ireland, where sheep were plucked instead of being shorn, ploughs were attached to a horse's tail and corn was burned to separate the grain from the straw.

[1]*The Irish Times* 12 December 1983